The Donkey: from N

The Donkey:
from Nose to Tail
Lorna Parker

In order of help, I would like to thank the following:

Elisabeth Svendsen MBE who personally showed me round and read through the sections I had written about her huge donkey sanctuary in Devon. Catherine Wolfe who proofread the whole draught text for me while on her maternity leave. My grandmother, Lady Whitelaw, and her brothers, Major Jock Sprot and Colonel Aidan Sprot, who provided both funds and photographs from the family album. Philip Doumler, a final year student at Cheltenham College in 2008, who drew all the cartoons. Janice Mather from Ben Cracknell Studios who patiently fielded many random emails and professionally designed the whole book.

Contents

Introduction

The donkey has been man's close friend and loyal ally for many centuries. Over the years it has come to be loved and pitied by many, but at the same time to symbolise stubbornness and stupidity. Why it has gained such a reputation is something of a mystery when one starts to look more carefully at the animal behind the image. If we can set aside for a moment our traditional and cultural attitudes we find a remarkably sure-footed, sensitive and intelligent beast that, in some ways, has evolved beyond recognition from its wild ancestor, the desert-dwelling African wild ass.

This book aims to reveal the truth behind the much-loved but much-maligned donkey – where did it come from, how do we explain its behaviour, how does it relate to humans and, indeed, how do we relate to it? What follows is not a manual for owners or a text-book for biologists, but an investigation into all aspects of an animal that seems at once so gentle and familiar yet has a history, a mythology and a nature that may surprise many.

How the Donkey got its Name

It seems fitting to start the tale of the donkey by looking at how and why it got its name. The word 'donkey' first appeared in print in the *Dictionary of the Vulgar Tongue* written by an army officer, Francis Grose, published in 1785. Many of Grose's terms are very vulgar indeed and were not included in the contemporary but more respectable work, Dr Johnson's *Dictionary of the English Language* published in 1755. 'Donkey, Donkey Dick' is defined by Grose as 'a he, or jack ass: called donkey perhaps, from the Spanish or don-like gravity of that animal, entitled also the king of Spain's trumpeter'. The word does not occur in Dr Johnson's work, indicating that he considered it slang and that the animal was more properly called an 'ass'. 'Ass' is indeed a very ancient English word that derives from the Latin name, *Equus asinus,* but to see how long 'donkey' has been in our language we must look at its most likely etymology.

Both 'donkey' and 'monkey', its only related word in English, with which it was at first pronounced to rhyme, are thought to be borrowings from Old Flemish. 'Donkey' may well have come from 'donnekijn', a Flemish term meaning 'little dun-coloured thing' and 'monkey' from 'monnekijn', a 'little monk'.

A second theory for the derivation of the word 'donkey' is that it came directly from the personal name 'Duncan'. In support of this, 'cuddy', the Scottish word for donkey, is thought to derive from 'Cuthbert'; 'neddy', an old familiar donkey name, from 'little Edward'; 'dobbin', referring to a steady old horse, from 'Robin', and 'jack' and 'jenny' are the respective names for the male and female donkey. Although it is unsure who the 'Duncan' concerned may have been, the connection between the donkey and the name, 'Cuthbert', is based on the fact that the animal was introduced to Northern Britain at about the same time as Christianity, and may have been spread by travelling monks from the cult of Cuthbert, Saint of Holy Island.

Throughout its history the donkey has been popularly viewed as a lowly and second-rate beast and has accordingly acquired a number of diminutive names. These often came from gypsies who trailed around the countryside spreading both donkeys and their jargon to new areas. 'Moke' is an old gypsy term which probably came from Welsh gypsies in whose language 'mokio' means an ass. 'Moke' was in common use in 19th century Britain when costermongers had their traditional 'moke and barrows' and is now often heard in the U.S. where the Press refer to miniature donkeys as 'minimokes'. The many feral donkeys that currently exist in America are popularly called 'burros' which is Spanish for 'donkey' and this is most often used in the Southern States which retain some Spanish influence.

CHAPTER 1

The Donkey's Origins

In order to find out where the donkey came from in biological terms, we need to look at its ancestry within the animal world. The donkey, as we know it, is a domesticated form of the wild ass and to get right back to its roots we need to see how this species evolved. The easiest way of tracking the origin of a wild animal is to refer to the natural classification system. This is a hierarchical system in which a few groups each containing many distantly related species of animal repeatedly branch into many groups each composed of fewer more closely related species. At the very top of the hierarchy is the whole animal kingdom and at the bottom are the millions of different individual species ranging from man to millipede.

It may help to understand the wild ass if we start by comparing it to our own species, Homo sapiens; and in order to see what we both have in common and thus how closely related we are, it is necessary to identify which groups in the classification system we both belong to, and how.

As we have just seen, at the top of the natural classification system's hierarchy is the largest group, containing all animal species – this is known

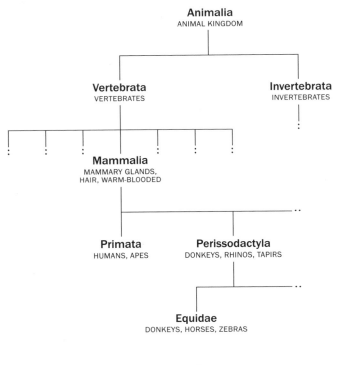

Animalia
ANIMAL KINGDOM

Vertebrata
VERTEBRATES

Invertebrata
INVERTEBRATES

Mammalia
MAMMARY GLANDS,
HAIR, WARM-BLOODED

Primata
HUMANS, APES

Perissodactyla
DONKEYS, RHINOS, TAPIRS

Equidae
DONKEYS, HORSES, ZEBRAS

FIGURE 1

as the **Animalia** (animal kingdom). All of its members share only the following two very basic features:

○ *An inability to make their own food from air and water and a need to feed on other organisms.* A wild ass sticks purely to the matter from the plant world whereas most humans also devour fellow animals.

○ *An ability to sense changes in the environment and respond by moving away from or towards them.* Man and wild ass are both attracted to and repelled by a huge range of stimuli but an ass can run away a lot faster than us.

At the second highest level in the hierarchy the **Animalia** subdivides into two distinct subgroups: **Vertebrata** (vertebrates) and **Invertebrata** (invertebrates). Wild ass and man both belong to the **Vertebrata**:

○ We both have an embryo with a flexible skeletal rod (the notochord) that, before birth, develops into a backbone. Those of us who have sat on a donkey's back know all about this.

At the next rank down in the classification system the **Vertebrata** branches into seven much smaller groups. These subgroups range from one containing highly developed animals such as ourselves to one containing organisms that have changed very little from their primitive, common ancestor such as jawless fish. Like man, the wild ass belongs to the most evolutionary-advanced group of vertebrates which is known as the **Mammalia** (mammals). There are, altogether, some 4250 different species of mammals, all with the following features:

○ *A warm-blooded body kept at a constant temperature.* Both man and wild ass have a body temperature of 36–38 °C which we maintain by sweating to cool down and by having a covering of hair to help in heat preservation. In the case of wild asses, this hairy coat grows thicker in winter when it is most needed – we just put on more clothes.

○ *Females which suckle their young on milk secreted from mammary glands.* Interestingly, donkey milk is closer in composition to human milk than that of any other animal. For this reason donkey milk was once used as a children's medicine and orphaned donkey foals are sometimes bottle-fed with human milk substitutes.

○ *The birth of live young*. This is true of all mammals apart from echidnas and duck-billed platypuses which lay eggs. Before being born, both man and ass embryos develop in the mother's womb for many months where they are nourished through a placenta. The average gestation period for a female donkey is a whole 11–12 months – 3 months longer than a woman.

○ *Two sets of specialised teeth*. The young of both man and ass grow a set of milk teeth that are shed and replaced by a combination of incisors, canines, premolars and molars that help us bite and chew efficiently. To deal with coarse plants, a donkey's teeth must be larger and higher crowned than our own and it can give a much more damaging bite, should it wish to do so, than a human.

○ *Ears containing three sound-conducting ear ossicles, or bones, in the middle section*. Although the ears of man and ass have a similar internal structure, our ear lobes are significantly different.

○ *A muscular diaphragm which separates the heart and lungs from the abdominal cavity*. Movement of the diaphragm assists us both in breathing and speaking and enables a donkey's voice to be projected somewhat further than our own.

○ *A lower jaw that is hinged directly to the skull*

○ *Mature red blood cells that lack a nucleus*

So far we have seen that, based on our common biological traits, both man and ass are classed as **Animalia** (animals), **Vertebrata** (vertebrates) and **Mammalia** (mammals). Below the level of **Mammalia** our differences outweigh our similarities and ass and man separate out into different subgroups. The group to which humans and their closest relatives, the apes and monkeys, belong is known as the **Primata** (primates). One feature that links primates together is manual dexterity which results from the possession of thumbs and big toes that face and can touch the other digits. The wild ass certainly does not have this and it, along with four species of rhinoceros, three of tapir, three of zebra and one of horse, fall into a group known as the **Perissodactyla** (perissodactyls). The traits that define this group are:

○ A *diet that consists solely of plants.* All perissodactyls are strictly herbivorous and feed either by grazing (cropping grass) or browsing (taking shoots and leaves from trees and bushes). Forest-dwelling tapirs and rhinoceroses feed much more on shrubs and trees than wild asses, zebras and horses that inhabit open grassy plains.

○ *High-crowned cheek teeth specially adapted for grinding tough plant matter.* Crushing up vegetation requires large molariform teeth and these range from the rather simple back teeth of the tapir to the ass's battery of specialised molar and pre-molars each with a thick deposit of enamel.

○ *An odd number of hooves on each leg.* Hooves are protective horny cases that form around what were once separate toes on a distant ancestor; animals which have them are known as ungulates. Ungulates are divided into two groups according to whether their hooves are entire or cloven (divided into two equal parts). The cloven hoofed group is known as the **Artiodactyla** and includes camels, pigs, cattle, antelope, goats and sheep. The **Perissodactyla**, to which the ass belongs, have an odd number of hooves on each foot – the wild ass, horse and zebra have, of course, just one while the rhinoceros has three.

○ *Large or medium in size.* Members of the **Perissodactyla** alive today range from the rounded, pig-sized tapir to the comparatively massive rhinoceros which can be up to 5 metres long and 2 metres tall. From the fossil record scientists have devised that a long extinct relative of the rhinoceros known as 'Baluchitherium' was the largest of all known land mammals standing about 5.5 metres high at the shoulder. At about 2.5 metres long and 1 metre high, wild asses are closer to the tapir.

○ *Fear of man.* Although domesticated horses and donkeys happily spend time with humans their wild ancestors and rest of the **Perissodactyla** avoid contact with man whenever possible. Rhinoceroses and wild asses have good reason to fear us, since we have driven them almost to extinction and they now only exist in game reserves and national parks. Wild horses and asses were once hunted and eaten by man, while rhinoceroses have long been hunted and killed for their valued horn.

○ *Communication made by calls and changes in facial expression.* All the **Perissodactyla** can snort and squeal. Donkeys also bray, horses and zebras whinny whilst rhinoceroses and tapirs are occasionally known to bellow and even to whistle. Facial expressions are well developed in horses, asses and zebras, which often live in groups and need to communicate a broad range of emotions. This is not the case with rhinoceroses and tapirs which are non-social animals leading largely solitary lives and requiring only a very limited range of visual signals.

○ *Occasional fighting.* The pattern of fighting in any species is related to the amount of bodily protection and weaponry it possesses. Fights amongst rhinoceroses follow a set pattern and consist of charges and strikes with horns. Donkeys may bite and kick when provoked but are gentle in comparison with zebras which are known to circle, neck fight, bite, kick and rear up.

Beneath the level of the **Perissodactyla**, the wild ass is placed into a small, select group known as the **Equidae** (equids) that is comprised solely of it and its two closest relatives, the horse and zebra. All equids have the following characteristics:

○ *Hooves that are made up of only one functional toe.* All equids alive today are thought to be descended from a single animal, a small terrier-sized creature called a **Hyracotherium** which had five separate digits on each foot. As they evolved from this common ancestor they all lost toes one and five and had toes two and four reduced to what are now 'splint bones' in their lower legs. What was once the third toe is the only one still to function as such and the hard casing around this, sometimes equated to a toenail, comprises the undivided hoof.

○ *Long legs that enable swift running.* An obvious feature that distinguishes equids from rhinos and tapirs is the length of their legs in proportion to their body size. Living on open plains means that zebras, wild asses and horses all need to be highly mobile to escape swift-footed predators and cover large distances to find food. They thus evolved long and slender legs which allow them to run faster and for longer than their forest-dwelling relatives. Horses are the fastest moving equids and can gallop at up to 65 km/hr.

○ *Chestnuts and ergots.* These are patches of very hard skin, thought to be vestiges of separate ancestral toes, found on the legs of all equids. Chestnuts, situated at knee-height, are normally found on all four limbs of the horse but only on the front legs of asses and zebras whereas ergots are located at the back of the foot and occur on all legs of all equids.

○ *An ability to interbreed.* Zebras, asses and horses can all interbreed with each other to produce hybrid offspring, though these are almost always sterile. As we shall see later, producing the mule, a cross between a male donkey and a female horse, has been one of the most important roles of the donkey throughout its history in man's world. The rare hybrid between the ass and various zebra species has been called zebroid, assbra, zebrule, zebrinny, zebryle, zebret but is more usually referred to as a zebronkey.

The Direct Ancestor – The Wild Ass

It is now time to look in more detail at the type of equid which directly gave rise to the domestic donkey: the wild ass. To help understand why the wild ass looks and behaves as it does we need to know what sort of environment it inhabits and then see how it has adapted to survive there. It may come as a surprise, considering how at home the donkey seems in lush, temperate Britain, to know that wild asses live in some of the most dry and inhospitable

The African Wild Ass (*Equus africanus*) – wild ancestor of the domestic donkey.

Quagga (*Equus africanus*), a zebralike equid of South Africa that is now extinct. Photograph taken in London Zoo between 1892 and 1907.

regions on earth. Very few, if any, remain in the wild today but those that do subdivide into two distinct groups: the African wild asses, or true asses, found on the margins of North African deserts, and the Asian wild asses, or half asses, spread over arid mountain plateaux of Mongolia and Tibet.

African Wild Asses (*Equus africanus*)

The African wild ass is a typical desert animal with long slender legs, a compact body, neat head and very long ears and is known as the 'true ass' because it is the most similar in size and shape to the domestic donkey. In 1845 Low reported that wild asses 'have been seen by many travellers, from the countries of the Red Sea to Cape Verde on the Atlantic; and they have been recently observed in great numbers about the cataracts towards the high lands of Bahr-el Ariad, or White Nile.' (**Low 1845: 437–444**) Today, however, African wild asses are critically endangered, if not extinct, in their native lands with any that do still exist being restricted to the Horn of Africa. (**Moehlman 2005:76–81**)

From the fossil record, scientists have determined that there were once about five different types of African wild ass spread in a continuous band across arid North Africa from the Atlas Mountains to the Red Sea. All are thought to have been subspecies of *Equus africanus* and included the following:

○ *Nubian wild ass* (*Equus africanus* '*africanus*') – this is believed now to be one of only two subspecies of African ass that, just possibly, still exists in the wild though it once ranged over the extensive mountainous semi-desert lands of Nubia and eastern Sudan. The last individuals to be seen alive were reputed to make the same noise as the domestic donkey and, occasionally, to bear the same marking of a cross on their backs.

○ *Somali wild ass* (*Equus africanus* '*somaliensis*') – this is the one other African ass subspecies that might still survive in the wild, though there have been no sightings of it since 1989 when a few hundred were seen in northern Somalia and the Danakil region of Ethiopia. Luckily, a small captive population is held in zoos and from these we know that the Somali wild ass is larger than its Nubian relative with a shoulder height of over 140 cm. Its coat turns from buff-grey in summer to iron-grey in winter and it has a strongly marked stripe along the back and well-marked horizontal bars around the lower legs.

○ *Eritrean wild ass* (***Equus africanus*** *'dianae'*) – this was described as a subspecies by Dollman in 1935. He reported it as having a long but poorly-marked shoulder stripe and faint traces of bands around the legs but, as nothing matching this description has been seen since, it may well have been a hybrid between the Nubian ass and the Somali ass. (Moehlman 2005:76–81)

Asian Wild Asses (*Equus hemionus*)

The Asian wild asses, also known as onagers or half-asses, are all thought to be different subspecies of *Equus hemionus*. Their appearance, half way between a horse and an African ass, means they are sometimes called 'half-asses' or 'stilt-legged asses'. Their coats vary from sandy yellow to reddish to pale buff with white underparts and they have no clearly defined body markings.

Although now critically endangered in the wild, Asian wild asses once roamed over a huge area of southwestern Asia from the lowland deserts of the Levant to the mountains of Tibet and Mongolia. Such a broad geographical range meant that a number of local races or subspecies evolved and these include the following:

○ *Syrian wild ass* (***Equus hemionus*** *'hemippus'*) – this became extinct in 1927 when the last recorded animal died in Vienna zoo. It was the smallest of the Asian asses, rarely more than 1 metre high at the shoulder, and had the shortest ears. It was also the subspecies found furthest west, inhabiting the alluvial plains of the Near East from the Levant to Mesopotamia, modern day Iraq, and is thought to be the wild ass of the Bible, with the Hebrew name 'pere'.

The Asian Wild Ass (*Equus africanus*).

○ *Tibetan wild ass or Onager (**Equus hemionus** 'onager')* – this is larger than the Syrian ass and can live at higher altitudes. The fossil record shows that it was once widespread but it was mercilessly hunted from the prehistoric period onwards and now only survives in captivity.

○ *Kulan (**Equus hemionus** 'kulan')* – sixty years ago this was close to extinction, surviving only in remote parts of Turkmenistan and Kazakhstan, but since then a major conservation effort meant that by 1992 its numbers had risen to more than 2,000. Following its translocation to other protected areas, it is now spread over a relatively large area covering Turkestan, North China, Mongolia and southeast Siberia. The kulan shows a large variation in colour and size but can be distinguished from other wild asses by its blunter nose and thicker skull. It is a very swift runner, reaching speeds of 64.4 km/h (40 mph) when running on the open plains.

○ *Indian wild ass or khur* (**Equus hemionus** 'khur') – only a small number of these now exist in a single population in a designated wild ass sanctuary in the desert of the Little Rann of Kutch in northern Gujarat. The subspecies was described in 1895 by Tegetmeier & Sutherland (Clutton-Brock, J 1992) who, in one passage, called it 'totally wild and untameable' and, in another, 'as docile as a tame donkey'.

○ *Kiang* (**Equus kiang**) – this has become so different from other Asian wild asses that it is often considered a separate species and is so rare that it is possibly now extinct in the wild. Kiangs are the largest of all the wild asses and, if they do still survive, live only at high altitudes, above 3000m, on the cold, dry grasslands of Tibet where they are preyed upon by wolves. They feed on grasses and low-lying plants that are plentiful only from August to October, so during this time they must eat determinedly and put on a thick layer of fat to help them survive the winter. Unfortunately their extra meat has meant kiangs have always been mercilessly hunted. For extra padding, they grow a thick and woolly winter coat that they rub off in spring by rolling on the ground. To obtain water during the dry season kiangs stay near streams and in winter, they need to break ice or eat snow. They are courageous animals, said to plunge unhesitatingly into raging mountain torrents to cross to the other side.

Although, as already mentioned, every subspecies of wild ass is critically endangered (if not extinct) in the wild, some still exist in zoos and national parks. The African asses are in the most urgent need of conservation as in 1992 their captive population numbered only about 70 animals, 31 of which were Somali wild asses and the rest of mixed origins. Asian wild asses are comparatively better protected; some 556 zoo animals were recorded in 1989 and others survive in protected Reserves. The kulan is the only subspecies that is currently thought to have a large enough population to ensure conservation of its genetic diversity. This means that, as things stand now, the kulan is the only wild ass adaptable enough to survive unprotected in the wild and without urgent conservation none of the others may ever again be found outside captivity.

Having looked in some detail at all the different types of wild ass, we can attempt to determine which one was the direct ancestor of the domestic donkey. All clues point to the African wild asses rather than their Asian counterparts. In terms of appearance, it is the African wild asses with their longer ears that are the most similar in size, colour and body markings to the donkey. When it comes to nature, African asses would probably have been easier to domesticate than Asian wild asses which are said to be too wild and irascible to control and habituate.

A study of the genes of the wild ass population also indicates that the African rather than the Asian asses are the donkey's progenitors, since they are the only ones with the same number of chromosomes as the domestic donkey and are thus able to interbreed with it to produce fertile offspring. In 2004, a detailed scientific analysis of DNA collected from donkeys in 52 countries and from wild asses in Africa and Asia showed that there are two distinct populations of domestic donkey, both of which are directly related to the African asses. One is clearly derived from the Nubian wild ass and the other is closer to the Somalian one, although it does not fall within the current genetic range of wild Somalian asses. The scientists concluded that donkeys were probably domesticated twice, once from each of the two African wild asses, or once from the Nubian ass and again from a now extinct subspecies of ass. (Beja-Pereira 2004:1781)

Over time, the difference between the wild and domestic forms of ass has become so great that they are now recognised as separate species and the donkey or domestic ass has been given the Latin name, *Equus asinus.* The transformation of the wild ass of Africa to the domestic donkey, able to live more than 1000 miles north if its parched home terrain in damp fields of northern Europe, must be one of the most remarkable examples of evolution within a domestic species. To see how great that transformation has been, we will look now at the domestic donkey and its place in today's world.

CHAPTER 2

The Donkey Population Today

Donkey Numbers and Distribution

The domestic donkey is now found in every continent of the world except Antarctica. In 2003 the global donkey population was thought to be about 40.3 million, most of which are kept in developing countries where they make useful pack and draught animals. The following tables, published by the Food and Agriculture Organisation (FAO), give an idea of the world-wide spread of donkeys:

World Population of donkeys by region (000s)

Region	1989–1991	2000	2001	2002	2003
World	43113	40923	40825	40395	40328
Africa	13659	13689	13655	13650	13667
North & Central America*	3688	3757	3773	3773	3779
S America	4016	4009	4028	4059	4094
Asia	20407	18663	18578	18141	18020
Europe	1030	796	781	764	759
Oceania†	9	9	9	9	9

* Mexico had approximately 86.4% of the donkeys of North and Central America in 2003
† The only countries listed for Oceania are Australia with 2F and Papua New Guinea with 7F
(*Food and Agriculture Organisation* 2003:207–209)

Countries with the most donkeys (000s)

Country	1989–1991	2000	2001	2002	2003
China	11129	9348	9227	8815	8499
Pakistan	3421	3800	3900	3900	4100
Ethiopia	3400F	3414	3414F	3430F	3430F
Mexico	3187F	3250F	3260F	3260F	3260F
Egypt	2356F	3050F	3050F	3050F	3070F
Iran	1911F	1600F	1600F	1600F	1600F
Brazil	1343	1242	1239	1250F	1250F
Nigeria	932F	1000F	1000F	1000F	1000F
India	960F	750F	750F	750F	750F

F = FAO Estimate
(*Food and Agriculture Organisation* 2003:207–209)

European Countries with the most donkeys (000s)

Country	1989–1991	2000	2001	2002	2003
Bulgaria	329	208	210	197	197F
Portugal	170F	135F	130F	130F	125F
Spain	127F	140F	140F	140F	140F
Albania	113*	113*	105*	105F	105F
Greece	137F	70F	68F	68F	68F
Romania	35F	30F	31F	28F	28F
Italy	69F	23F	23F	23F	23F
Russian Fed	22F	20F	20F	20F	
France	21F	16F	16F	15F	15F
UK	12*	12F	11F	12F	

* Unofficial Figure
F = FAO Estimate
(*Food and Agriculture Organisation* 2003:207–209)

The figures given above include all donkeys irrespective of age, place or purpose of breeding but they should be treated as rough guides as most countries consider donkeys 'uneconomic' and may well underestimate their true numbers.

In any area, the number of donkeys in relation to humans can be used as an indicator of the animal's economic importance and the following table gives the donkey to human ratios for 2001:

Donkey to Human Ratios

Region	Donkeys (000s)	Humans (000s)	Donkey:Human Ratio
World	40395	6224978	1:154
Africa	13650	832089	1:61
South America	4059	357329	1:88
Asia	18141	3775948	1:208
Europe	764	727019	1:951
Bolivia	632	8645	1:14
Mexico	3260	101965	1:31
China	8815	1302307	1:148
France	15	59850	1:3990
UK	11	52987	1:4817
USA	52	291038	1:5597

(Food and Agriculture Organisation 2003:207–209)

Donkey in its extreme of a hard Scottish winter, ca 1930.

Population Demography

In any area, the ratio of male to female or young to old donkeys will depend largely on the value attributed to them by society. In places such as the Darfur, an agro-pastoral region of western Sudan, where male and female donkeys are used indiscriminately and there is no off-take for slaughter or sales, the population structure probably represents one of the most natural ones of all domestic animals. The ratio of males to females is roughly 1:1 and depends entirely on the birth rate and longevity of individual animals.

In the Air region of northern Niger, however, where selling donkeys generates additional income, there are relatively more females as males fetch a higher price and are sold off. In 1982 only 30 per cent of donkeys found here were male (Wilson and Wagenaar 1982). The situation was seen to be reversed in urban areas of Mali, where the donkeys are bought in and used solely for work. As male donkeys were considered stronger they made up over 85 per cent of the total population in 1978. (Wilson 1978:183–189)

Feral Donkeys

Having looked at the wild ass in its natural environment and at the donkey in captivity, we can now turn our attention to animals that fit into neither category; donkeys which were once domestic but have escaped into the wild and gone feral. Feral donkeys now exist in a number of countries and can be a serious menace as their overgrazing of marginal grasslands causes soil erosion, habitat destruction and unacceptable competition with livestock and native wildlife. Donkeys can survive well as feral animals as they feed on ubiquitous grasses, have the resilience to survive in extreme temperatures and, once away from human control, can move fast over long distances to reach new areas. In one instance, a donkey, thought to have been abandoned 18 years before by its owner, was found alive and well on an uninhabited island off the west coast of Ireland. It had managed to survive on its own but appeared quite happy to be rescued and to live as a pet in human society once again. If they are fed, rather than hunted, by man, feral donkeys can indeed soon become tame again, but tend to be quite importunate.

As well as stealing the best grass, feral donkeys in arid areas will deprive native wild animals of scarce water, since they are less fearful of man and so are more willing to approach water troughs. When their populations are limited only by the availability of food and water, some feral donkeys become thin and diseased, leading to widespread public disapproval. Their unsightly appearance, and damage which they cause to fragile ecosystems, means there is a continual need to control their numbers. In the early days this was done by shooting them indiscriminately from aircraft or motor vehicles or polluting their watering holes. Although most excess feral animals are now killed through strictly regulated government roundups, a technical manual to disseminate safe, humane and efficient methods of culling is long overdue.

The largest populations of feral donkeys, numbering many thousands, are found on the open plains of the Western United States and in the Australian outback. In the US, feral donkeys are called burros and mostare probably descended from pack animals that were lost or abandoned by their owners with the coming of the railways in the 19th century. Along with mustangs, their horse equivalent, burros quickly became so numerous that they were later cleared from prairie lands in an effort to preserve water and grazing for livestock and most are now found in more inhospitable, mountainous areas. In Death Valley, where burros are descended from donkeys belonging to early prospectors and miners, they are the largest animal able to survive in the wild and have become a serious threat to the native flora and fauna. Some are shot by game wardens to preserve stocks of mountain goats and big-horn sheep. Burros do have some natural enemies in the area, such as the occasional puma or mountain lion, which will attack very young and vulnerable animals. Even a juvenile feral donkey is quite a match for a puma, however, and a healthy foal is rarely caught.

Despite conservationists' efforts to restrict numbers of feral donkeys, both the International Society for the Protection of Mustangs and Burros (ISPMB) and the Wild Free-Roaming Horse and Burro Act, passed in 1971, work to safeguard all feral equids. The ISPMB, based in America, has secured a 3,000,000 acre reserve for burros in California while the Act affords full-scale protection to feral equids on all public lands.

A popular way to reduce numbers of destructive feral donkeys is to capture them and then give them to people to keep as pets. To this end, the American Bureau of Land Management now runs an adoption process to match unwanted burro with willing owners. The 'Adopt-a-Horse or Burro Program' was launched nationwide in 1976 and since then, more than 150,000 wild horses and burros have been adopted. Under the scheme, the federal government remains the legal custodian of the animals for one year and checks are made to see if it is being properly treated. The cost of adoption for a burro in 1980 was $75.00, $200.00 for a horse, and this covers a health certificate, brand inspection fees and transportation from point of capture to the distribution centre. One Texan, Jet O Lewis, who adopted three wild burros described the process of 'gentling' them. He first put them in a sturdy corral and fed them little and often. After two weeks he could use a curry comb on two of them and the third was almost ready for currying. Within four weeks, two would eat from his hand and he turned them into a pasture and started a daily training program. In a matter of months, all three burros would follow him round the pasture and, in his own words, 'my wife and I have truly found that happiness is adopting a wild burro'. (Hutchins, B & P 2002)

In Australia, many thousands of feral donkeys are held responsible for soil erosion and the degradation of large areas of pasture. In 1942 several hundred of them were captured, broken to work and then sent to Papua New Guinea to contribute to the war effort but this did little to dent their population and by the 1950s around 150,000 were living wild. During the 1960s about 28,000 feral donkeys were reportedly shot on the Victoria River Downs Station but they still thrive far too well in the outback and in 1982 an aerial survey recorded 65,755 animals on 111,400 km^2 (there were 533,786 domestic cattle and 55,022 feral horses over the same area). Feral donkeys were found living in small groups of an average 4.2 head although herds of 150–200 head were not uncommon. (Wilson 1990: 581–601)

The only record of a long established population of island-dwelling feral donkeys was made on Socotra, which lies 193 kilometres east of the tip of the Horn of Africa. Feral asses were first seen on the island in 1898–1899 and described as being very small and mouse-coloured with a dark shoulder stripe and faint bars around their legs. Their uniformity of size and colour indicated that they had been on the island for many generations and had not interbred with domestic donkeys. Forbes (1903) considered that the Socotran asses more closely resembled the Nubian wild ass than the Somali ass, which would have been geographically closer, and thought that they were probably descended from animals that were taken there by the ancient Egyptians or Romans. If this population of feral asses still survives on Socotra it could be an invaluable genetic relic of the now, quite possibly, extinct Nubian wild ass.

Any Nubian wild asses left in the wild are certainly threatened with extinction and one of the species' most dangerous enemies is, ironically, the feral donkey. Feral donkeys, of which there are quite a few in Africa, can interbreed with African wild asses to produce fertile hybrids. Too much hybridisation between the two species will change the gene pool of the wild ass and eradicate it from the wild for ever.

In the feral donkey's favour, it can be said that the selective pressures they have endured in the wild are likely to have shaped them genetically, producing stock more hardy than domestic animals'. They could therefore prove a useful genetic resource and should be preserved. A survey of the genetics of feral donkey populations worldwide is now needed in order to identify objectively those of importance for the conservation of genetic diversity. (Duncan 1992)

CHAPTER 3

The Complete Donkey

Anatomy

Most donkeys stand somewhere between 102–142 cm high at the shoulder, although this can vary considerably, from 173 cm for the male Poitou ass down to just 61 cm for a female miniature donkey. In proportion to the rest of the body, donkeys' backs and ears are long and their croups or rumps are relatively short.

Donkeys range in colour from black to white, through every shade of grey and brown and some are even pink, which is correctly known as pale strawberry roan. Chestnut is very rare, as is floral-white; the only known floral-white donkeys live semi-wild in a nature reserve on Sardinia. Multi-coloured and spotted animals, usually black and white, are uncommon though in the Ethiopian Rift Valley they constitute about 3 per cent of the population. Almost universally, the donkey bears a cross on its back made up of a dark stripe from mane to tail, known as an eel stripe, and a shorter one across its shoulders. Its mane is short and upright and its tail, with long

PHOTOGRAPHED BY SHELAGH POWELL, 2003

The donkey: nose to tail.

hairs at the end only, is more cow-like than horse-like. One of its most distinctive features is its very long ears which are dark at the base and tip. Compared to other equids, the donkey has a disproportionately large head with a prominent forehead – this makes it a particularly poor swimmer.

As we have already seen, the donkey, in common with the horse and zebra, has one functional toe on each foot that takes the form of a single hard hoof. Its legs are shorter and more slender than those of other equids, which makes it slower and not as strong weight for weight. The donkey's upright shoulder also acts to reduce its speed as it is unable to lift its feet very high, so it has a rather shuffling gait, especially when trotting.

As previously described, all equids have areas of horny skin known as chestnuts and ergots, both vestiges of ancestral toes, on their legs. One clear cut anatomical difference between donkeys and horses is that donkeys have chestnuts on their forelegs only whereas horses have them on all four limbs.

The donkey's staple food, grass, contains hard particles of silica in its cell walls which make it difficult to break down into digestible form. To deal with this, the donkey has developed a formidable battery of teeth consisting of sharp incisors or nippers to bite and pull grass into the mouth and high crowned molar teeth to crush it down. Situated in between the incisors at the front of the mouth and molars at the back are the canines or tushes (tusks) whose main use is in fighting and grooming. These are quite large in the male but very small or even absent in the female and, when used in conjunction with the incisors, can give a fearsome bite.

As in humans, for the first four or five years of its life a donkey has a set of milk teeth which are then shed and replaced by permanent ones. Attentive owners have noted that the cast milk teeth are rarely found in the field or stable and it is therefore assumed the donkey swallows them. The permanent adult teeth have crowns that carry on growing throughout the animal's natural lifespan to compensate for their continual wear through grazing. Domestic donkeys given an easy life tend to live much longer than they would in the wild and elderly animals can sometimes starve to death as they are unable to eat properly when their teeth finally stop growing. Generally speaking, a donkey's teeth grow slightly faster than they wear and as they continue to grow their angle of eruption changes. An older animal can have abnormally long, prominent teeth which gives rise to the expression: 'long in the tooth'.

Understanding the growth of a donkey's teeth can help many owners who may be unsure of their donkey's age. As with a horse, it is possible to estimate how old a donkey is by examining the pattern of wear and growth of its six bottom incisors. This can be fairly accurate up until the age of 20 but beyond that the process becomes less reliable as the teeth will stop growing. The method of aging an equid by looking at its teeth has given rise to the old saying, 'always look a gift horse in the mouth' – an animal over 20 would not be such a generous present.

Along with other equids, the donkey has a gap in its jaw between the molars at the back and the tushes and incisors at the front. This is the diastema which serves to lengthen the animal's face so that when it lowers its head to feed, its eyes are still at a height where they can watch for anything approaching. For wild asses grazing on open plains, a diastema enabled them to escape from predators. In the domestic donkey it is most useful to their human handlers as it is where the bit is placed. The diastema also provides humans with a relatively safe way of prising open a donkey's mouth. To reduce the chance of being bitten, fingers should be carefully slid in at the corner of the donkey's lips until they connect with the diastema and then the jaws can be gently forced apart.

Compared to other equids, the donkey has a relatively rough and woolly coat which means it is better able to survive in cold, mountainous regions. Although light rain will simply run off it, a donkey's coat does not have sufficient protective oils to repel a really hard downpour and it will soak up excess water like blotting paper. A sodden animal can take a while to get dry again and for this reason donkeys are not well suited to very wet environments and can appear more reluctant than horses to enter pools and rivers. Surprisingly, snow is less of a problem for a donkey than rain, since snowflakes that settle on its back may provide it with an extra layer of warmth.

Nutrition

The donkey has an efficient digestive system capable of breaking down the very coarsest of plant materials. The process of digestion starts in the mouth where food is crushed by the teeth and mixed with saliva to assist its passage to the stomach. Once in the stomach, digestive juices are added to the mixture to speed decomposition and these are enhanced by specialised micro-organisms released from a sac-like structure known as the caecum. The caecum is highly developed in the donkey and contains more digestive agents than are found in other herbivores of its size. After the various gut micro-organisms have decomposed the food mixture, the process of absorbing nutrients from it can begin. Sugars, starch, protein and fats are all digested and absorbed in the small intestines and the remaining roughage and fibre in the large intestines. Again, both these structures are well developed in the donkey compared with other sizeable herbivores and present a large surface area over which nutrient adsorption takes place. On leaving the intestines the remaining mixture, now the consistency of pea soup, passes into the rectum where water is removed and droppings formed.

The donkey's digestive system is well equipped to deal with plants that other animals would find insufficiently nutritious to be worth eating. The coarse nature of its diet, however, does mean the donkey has to eat a large amount to gain adequate nutrition and this results in its food passing rapidly through it.

It is not known how much a domestic donkey actually consumes but on a body weight basis it is thought to need only about 75% of that required by a horse. When left to graze naturally, donkeys spend about 50–55% of the day eating, 20% resting, 20% standing alert and 5–10% moving around the grazing area (Fielding, D & Krause, P 1998). The 'resting' period can be taken up either by dozing/sleeping or by 'loafing', which involves lazy self-comforting behaviour such as stretching, yawning, scratching, rubbing, grooming, rolling and shaking. Loafing tends to occupy much of the daytime in summer when it may be too warm for eating.

Wild asses had to travel over long distances to find enough to eat and needed to retain a healthy appetite to make the most of what food they found. For domestic donkeys that spend all day in a field of lush grass, the high appetite of their wild ancestors is a problem as they easily eat to excess and become overweight. Their tendency for indulgence has long been recognised by owners and dreaming of a donkey is said to denote satiated appetites, resulting from licentious excesses. Mules and donkeys are, however, less likely than horses to overeat and most can self-feed without as great a risk of obesity.

Reproduction

A donkey mare can bear her first foal at about one year old and may then remain sexually active well in excess of 20 years. She will have an oestrus cycle lasting 21–28 days during which the heat period is 2–7 days. In tropical areas, where there are no distinct seasons, oestrus may occur at any time of year but in temperate regions there is usually a well-defined breeding period, ensuring the foals are borne in spring.

The gestation period for a donkey can vary between 11 and 13 months and only one foal is borne at a time. A mare much prefers to foal on her own and if disturbed when going into labour is capable of holding on for another 3 days. The foal is born in a complete membrane sac of amniotic fluid with its hoofs completely covered in a rubbery substance that protects the mother. It breaks free from the sac within a few moments and soon struggles to stand and take its first unsteady steps. The mother licks her wet newborn to help stimulate her milk flow and then gently nudges it round to find her teat. It is vital that the foal receives its mother's milk as this contains antibodies that will protect it over its first days. Donkey foals are incredibly active and soon able to gallop speedily alongside their mothers. The mare is very protective of her young and the two will play and groom each other so forming a strong bond that can last till the end of the suckling period which may be up to six months.

Water Retention

The donkey has inherited from its desert-dwelling ancestor a camel-like ability to regulate its water content. The following physiological traits enable it to do this:

○ Ability to withstand a wide fluctuation in body temperature. A donkey's normal deep body temperature is about 36.4°C but up to 39.3°C been recorded for donkeys in the tropics. (Wilson 1990: 581–601) In allowing its temperature to rise slightly during the heat of the day, a donkey minimises the amount of water lost through sweating and during the night can dissipate heat to return its temperature to normal.

○ Ability to sweat/shiver. Sweating and shivering are both ways for an animal to return its body temperature to normal, should it become too cold or hot respectively. The sooner it can do this, the less water it will lose through evaporation and donkeys are effective at both. They have sweat glands all over their body so can lose heat rapidly by sweating and they can increase the warming effect of shivering by also erecting their body hair.

○ Ability to control drinking and urinating. After a period of drought a donkey can drink 24-30 litres of water in 2–5 minutes to restore its normal water content quickly and can take in up to 98% of its original live weight in 10 minutes without over-hydration. When feeling dehydrated a donkey minimises water loss by eating less and therefore losing less water via the faeces. The amount of water lost through urination is relatively low even when it is allowed to drink freely.

Life Span

The average life expectancy of a donkey varies greatly according to where it lives. In the UK it averages 27 years but in Africa it is more like 11. Donkeys in Developed Countries can live till their 60s – 'donkey's years' indeed – but, ironically, longevity is one of their main problems as they may well outlive their owners and so lose their home. The situation is even worse for mules, which can survive for up to 70 years.

'Not for donkey's years' meaning not for ever so long is a pun on donkey's ears which are notoriously long. However, the donkey's long life span has given rise to a number of adages and, according to Sam Weller in Charles Dickens's *Pickwick Papers*, a dead donkey is one of the two things that no man ever see, the other being a dead post-boy!

Two friendly donkeys grooming each other.

Bonding and Friendship

Both wild asses and domestic donkeys form friendships by playing with, nuzzling and grooming each other. Grooming involves two animals simultaneously stretching their heads forward to scratch the other's withers with their teeth.

The only strong bonds formed between wild asses are those between a mare and her foal. A Speed, writing in 1697, considered, 'there is in this creature [the ass], a great love towards her young; for if it be in danger, and cry out for help, she will not stick, if possible, to run through a circling fire to it.' (Speed ca.1697:100–103) A filly wild ass foal will usually stay with her mother for about 6 months, until she is old enough to foal herself, but colts may remain with their dams for several years. When they eventually leave, young colts tend to join together into small nomadic bachelor groups but friendships within the group are short-lived as each is seeking to beat the others to a mare in season, and to establish his own breeding territories. In areas falling outside a wild ass stallion's defined territory, males from the group may gather around available mares and fight over them.

Unless they are stallions with a female in the vicinity, in which case they would fight to the death, domestic donkeys will usually enjoy each others' company and form strong friendships. If a large number of donkeys are kept in the same field, those of a similar age will tend to get on best as younger ones may bully their elders. Bonds are strongest between pairs of donkeys and if members of a pair are separated each will tend to bray loudly and become very restless. Donkeys are known to mourn the death of a long-time companion and will become stressed and even aggressive if they see their companion being anaesthetised. (Rees 1993:103–107)

Donkeys have a variable reaction to other animals. They make the best of friends for a wide range of hoofed stock, seemingly having a particular liking for horses. Donkeys often have a calming effect on animals around them and the racehorse trainer, Jack O'Donoghue, kept them at his stables as he found they pacified his highly-strung thoroughbreds. One small landowner who managed to keep one horse, two ponies, a donkey, llamas, sheep, a goat, geese plus stray bantams on just four acres reckoned that it was his donkey, plus a plentiful supply of food, that prevented all war from breaking out. In his own words, 'The donkey helps. He's an old gelding – well over 30 – and he's a calming influence on the others. He's hardly done a day's honest work in all those years but he does seem to be a peace-maker. Every one of the animals in the field thinks he is their special friend. The sheep like him particularly, as he chases off stray dogs.' Another owner who kept their donkey in the same field as a llama found that the two became close friends and after the llama died the donkey sometimes rolled on its grave.

One animal that many donkeys do not interact well with is a dog, or any of its relatives, and some donkeys may chase things smaller than themselves such as cats and geese. As we shall see later, their dislike for dogs can mean donkeys make good guard animals. When it comes to humans, however, most well treated donkeys are very friendly and this, apparently, applies to our relatives as a monkey has been known to spend time preening a donkey.

The belief that donkeys understand humans well enough to be a reasonable judge of character has meant that dreaming of being kicked by one indicates that you are carrying on illicit connections from which you will suffer much anxiety from fear of betrayal. To dream of being thrown from a donkey denotes ill luck and disappointment in secular affairs, for example, lovers will quarrel and separate. (Parker 2007)

Aggression and Violence

As wild asses inhabited arid regions that could support very few other large animals, they rarely had to compete for resources and did not need an aggressive nature. Domestic donkeys are also, generally, non-combatant, being content to abandon the best grazing rather than fight over it. Donkey stallions, however, can become very violent when sexually aroused and extremely aggressive when running in a herd. Biting, rearing up and kicking out with the back legs are all employed as effective fighting actions.

Seeing and Hearing

Wild asses evolved good vision and a keen sense of smell in order to avoid predators on open plains. Though their survival no longer depends on it, domestic donkeys are still able to react surprisingly quickly to any threat or enticement – they certainly have a good sense of smell as stallions are able to detect mares in heat from an impressively long way away.

Vision is the most direct link to their environment that all higher animals possess and the donkey's close relative, the horse, has the largest eyes of any land mammal. As in the horse, the eyes of a donkey are set on the side of its head where they can together take in the entire horizon, including almost the whole area directly to the rear.

Donkeys unhappy at being taken through water, ca 1890.

When it comes to hearing, the bray of a donkey can carry two miles and its big ears may have evolved to hear over such distances – the smaller, rounded ears of a horse cannot do that. Another possible reason for the wild ass acquiring such long ears is so that they could be used as cooling aid. Other desert-dwelling animals such as the desert fox, desert rat and elephant have also evolved large ears and in the case of elephants, blood leaving the ears is up to 9°C cooler than when it enters them.

The donkey's famously prominent ears led one 17th century writer to offer the following somewhat picturesque theory regarding the animal's peculiar drinking habits: *'when they drink, they do it so mannerly, as if they were afraid to touch it with their lips* [...] *seeing the shadow of their goodly large ears in the water, in which they take great pride, they are offended, and suddenly draw back, as fearing they are wetted.'* (Speed ca.1697:100–103)

Donkey Talk

The majority of animals that produce sound through the mouth do so during exhalation – not the donkey. For some reason donkeys have the ability and the ardour to vocalise on both the inward and outward breath and their bray consists of two syllables, an inspiratory 'Ee' followed by an expiratory 'Aw' – 'screech, honk' is one way of describing it. Compared to most other evolutionary advanced animals, donkeys have a rather limited vocal repertoire but they can communicate through grunts, growls, snorts and whuffles.

In the case of wild asses most braying is done by territorial males trying to attract females. They tend to bray regularly after dawn and are sometimes answered by a potential mate. In equids that live in herds, the male boss of a harem will bray to communicate with his females or to round them up before moving to new location. Mares and foals rarely bray unless separated from each other or responding to other brays.

When kept alone domestic donkeys will bray in an attempt to locate others and loud and persistent braying indicates that a donkey is stressed because of fear or loss of contact with other donkeys. A donkey's cry is a long-distance communication signal that can carry and be heard over two miles and its low pitch means it travels far across open spaces. Stallions have the loudest bray, though they are considered rather tuneless, and in Mexico donkeys living at high altitudes were once called 'mountain canaries'.

A donkey's bray is certainly a quite extraordinary and instantly recognisable sound. The American President, George Washington, thought it a 'melodious utterance' and nicknamed the animal 'The King of Spain's Trumpeter' – his first donkey was a present from the Spanish. The poet, Ted Hughes, described 'the joke he seems always just about to tell me. And the laugh, the rusty, pump-house engine that cranks up laughter from some long-ago, far-off, laughter-less place – the dry hideous guffaw that makes his great teeth nearly fall out'. One children's book referred to it more simply as a 'funny, excited, croaky voice' (Goodall (1944) *Donkey's Glory*) and another reckoned that at the nativity, 'the shy little donkey was afraid his bray was too loud' (Tafuri (2002) *The Donkey's Christmas Song*)

A devoted donkey owner who wrote a novel based on time spent with his pets noted how his donkeys would bray in response to the foghorns of passing boats. His mare would 'emit the excruciating warble which was her speciality, a wailing saw, a falsetto groan' and her young foal 'followed in a more dignified manner; a real genuine hee-haw, in fact a whole series of hee-haws rising to a crescendo then descending again until it ended quietly in a grunt.' Tangye (1965: 103) The author goes on to eloquently describe how his donkeys had: *other more subtle forms of communication than their bellows. The snort was a joyous affair much used when they were released in a meadow they hadn't been in for a while; a scamper, a kicking of heels, a friendly dash at each other, heads down and snorts. It was a rich sound. A quick roll of bass drums. A proclamation that they were happy. At other times, I fear, the snort was only a tickle in the nose, grass seeds in a nostril; and then they would stand looking at us by a gate, or peering down at us from the field above the cottage, shaking their heads and snorting, as if they were blaming us for their temporary vexation.*

A persuasive, eloquent sound was their whimper. There was nothing obsequious about it. It was a means of making known the fact they had observed us pass by and would appreciate attention or a titbit. They would stand side by side, Penny's white nose topping Fred's white nose, trilling away like birds in a bush; and when we responded, when we advanced towards them speaking words of affection, they changed their whimper into a series of rapid sigh-like sounds. A rush of breath through their nostrils. A curious puffing method, it seemed, of saying thank you. (Tangye 1965:103–104)

In country lore the braying of a donkey has been said to presage rain or hail: 'It is time to lock your hay and corn, when the old donkey blows his horn'. There may have been some truth in this as the desert-dwelling wild ass must been aroused at the prospect of water.

A passage from *Physiologus*, an ancient text possibly written sometime between the 2nd and 5th centuries, describes another reason for the wild ass's call: 'when 25 days of March have passed, it [the wild ass] brays twelve times in the night and the same number in the day. From this the season is recognized as the 'Equinox' and people can tell, hour by hour, the time of day or night by counting the brays of the ass.' (White 1956: 82–83)

A wild ass's bray also has more sinister connotations as 'the breath of the Wild Ass, or Typhon' was said to bring bad dreams, murderous inclinations and rapes. Typhon was the younger child of Mother Earth and was considered 'the largest monster ever born.'

However enticing a donkey's bray appears to others of its kind, it seems that most humans have never taken to it. Such a hideous noise led to the belief that the animal must be tone deaf and the saying 'the ass is deaf to music'. Dreaming of a donkey braying in your face is said to denote that you are about to be publicly insulted by a lewd and unscrupulous person and hearing a distant, melancholy braying is thought to mean that you will receive wealth and release from unpleasant bonds by the death of someone close. A donkey owner may find that its noise rivals the peacock as a cause of social embarrassment and, although its bray might be part of the atmosphere in a Greek village, in rural Britain its ability to wake everyone within a mile is not much appreciated.

Body Language

A donkey's mood can be judged from its ears: interested if they are pricked forward; irritated if laid back. Laying back its ears is about the only way a donkey involved in a fight can protect the soft skin just behind them and in all equids this is used as a sign of aggression. Tail flicking (one way to get rid of flies) and pulling the mouth back, (ready to bite) are other clear-cut threatening gestures and, once again, it is best to move quickly. Wrinkling the nose (irritation) and drooping the lower lip (relaxation) are more subtle expressions and may only be observed at close quarters.

A donkey may express contentment by grooming either itself or a companion and investigating anything new. Eating things other than grass, such as soil or bushes, may indicate boredom and rolling may signal either pleasure or pain.

One experienced donkey owner, Derek Tangye, whose understanding of his donkeys' various forms of vocal communication has been described above, reckoned that:

An eloquent feature of the donkeys was their stare; and we never succeeded in growing accustomed to it. It was a weapon they used in morose moments of displeasure. There they would stand side by side in a meadow steadfastly watching us, exuding disapproval, condemning us for going about our business and not theirs. ... 'Why can't we go to another meadow?' 'I'd like a walk.' 'Oh dear, what is there to do?'

PHOTOGRAPHED BY JONATHAN LEACH

Donkey tolerating anti-fly device.

And when finally we relented, yielding to the influence of the stare, and dropped whatever we were doing, and decided to entertain him, Fred would look knowingly at Penny.
'Here they come, Mum. We've done it.' (Tangye 1965: 85)

As has already been mentioned, the act of rolling can signal both contentment and displeasure and here are Derek Tangye's evocative descriptions:

Fred's roll in the snow, however, was purely a gesture of joy. He was captivated by the feeling of the powdery stuff, and he rolled this way and that snorting with pleasure, kicking his heels in the air, and when he had had enough and stood up again, he looked as if he were a donkey wrapped in cotton wool. He then hoped for a game. Ears pinned back, head on one side, one could sense he was laughing at the huge joke of it all. (Tangye 1965: 132)

In contrast to her foal, Fred's, carefree rolling:

Penny [Tangye's donkey mare], like a fat lady on the seashore, had to watch her dignity when she followed suit. She would collapse to her knees, fall over to one side, then begin to wriggle this way and that in an endeavour to complete a roll. It was an embarrassing sight. She would get on her back, a huge grey barrel facing up to the heavens, then miserably fail to force herself over. Nor would her attempts be silent. She, like Fred, accompanied her efforts with repetitive, body-shaking grunts. A desperate sound, like a wrestler in combat; and when, if we were watching, she at last succeeded in making it by a final glorious lurch, Jeannie and I would send up a cheer. She would then get up, turn her back on us, stare at an imaginary interest in the distance, and pretend that nothing whatsoever untoward had happened. (Tangye 1965: 131–132)

In general, Tangye noted that:

The roll, in normal circumstances, was a solemn ritual. The ceremony was performed on a small circular patch in a carefully chosen position and, as it was well worn, the ground was either dusty or muddy according to the weather. This however, had no bearing on the success of the ceremony, for the roll was a donkey bath; and whether Fred rose from his roll in a cloud of dust or caked in mud, he was satisfied. As far as he was concerned he was clean. He had had his wash. (Tangye 1965: 131)

Learning and Intelligence

To increase their chances of survival donkeys, like all other living organisms, must learn to react in the most advantageous manner to specific actions or events. Their reaction may be either an instinctive reflex response or a voluntary one. An example of a reflex response is a donkey flinching when it hears a rustling sound in the bushes – it may initially have done this when a dog rushed out of the undergrowth and thereafter automatically associates any rustling sound with potential danger and reacts to this rather than the dog itself. A typical voluntary response in a donkey is to put its nose in a bucket: it has learnt from experience that this may hold food.

Learning always involves habituation, a process whereby an animal works out just which of the many stimuli it perceives are worth responding to and which should be ignored – it may be wise to jump at a crashing noise heard in the bushes, but it is foolish to react every time a leaf rustles in the wind. Much of the early training of a donkey involves habituating it to stimuli, such as a weight placed on its back, which it will initially find frightening but eventually learn to accept.

Some people relate intelligence in an animal to the speed at which it learns to react in what they consider a correct manner to new stimuli. The issue is not so straightforward, however, as a really intelligent animal may learn from experience that the reaction a human may want may not result in its own best interests. Not carrying out a desired response, i.e. refusing to be led towards a stable and thereby receiving a sugar lump, is not necessarily a sign of an animal being 'stupid' but quite possibly of intelligence; it may have learnt to associate being led towards a stable with being put in harness.

A donkey's reputation for stubbornness can therefore be seen as a misinterpretation of its highly-developed sense of self preservation. It is certainly difficult to force or frighten an animal into doing something it sees as disadvantageous and Carol Morse of the Donkey Breed Society reckons that a donkey's non-co-operation

means it is thinking about what it is being asked to do. Two other donkey experts appear to back up this claim: in the words of Robin Borwick, Founder of the Donkey Breed Society, 'a donkey's intelligence is far superior to that of a horse. This is what makes a donkey so irritating when he will not do what you tell him. A horse understands and obeys, or does not understand and requires further training, but a donkey, who knows perfectly well what is wanted, will only do what he considers is really needed'. (Borwick 1981) According to Dr Elisabeth Svendsen, Founder of the Donkey Sanctuary, 'if a horse naps when its gets to a puddle you can beat it and eventually it will go, but a donkey will not unless you walk in front and demonstrate that the water is shallow. As the saying goes: "You can beat a horse but you must negotiate with a donkey".' (Svendsen 1986)

One example of a horse appearing to outwit a donkey is in how it deals with snow. A horse is, apparently, much quicker to paw aside a layer of snow to get to the grass underneath than a donkey. This difference in behaviour could be due to the fact that the donkey's wild ancestors, unlike those of a horse, would never have encountered snow or it could be that the donkey realises that if it waits long enough it will be fed by an obliging human.

Certainly the donkey has not always been considered intelligent and according to the 12th century Latin Bestiary, 'people captured the Donkey by the following stratagem. Being forsooth a tardy beast and having no sense at all, it surrendered as soon as men surrounded it!'

Categories and Breeds of Donkey

Hundreds of years of selective donkey breeding by man in a wide variety of environments has resulted in a number of different forms of the animal. In much of the world, lack of attention to animal husbandry means there is little real difference between the donkey population and it can only be divided into rough categories. In developed countries, however, more care has been taken to produce healthy, good-looking individuals and a number of distinct breeds have been created. Since most donkeys fall into the rough categories it is these we will consider first and the following broadly recognisable types can be found in separate geographical regions:

○ 'Muscat', 'Syrian' or 'Arab' donkeys – these are found in Egypt (particularly in Upper Egypt), Sudan and along the coasts of enya and Tanzania. They are tall animals, averaging 123cm at the withers, which can move at high speed. Most have white or silver-grey hair and a black skin and in Middle Eastern countries the pure white animals are particularly favoured and have long been used for ceremonial purposes. Being relatively fast means Muscat donkeys are popular riding animals but their poor temperament and lack of stamina means that they are not suitable for packing or pulling carts.

○ Sudanese 'riding donkeys' – these have been developed in Sudan through selective breeding within the local donkey population although there may well have been some out-crossing to the Muscat donkey just described. They are generally impressive looking animals, standing about 112–120 cm at shoulder height, with long ears and a coat varying from white to black. Like Muscat donkeys, they are used almost exclusively for riding and seldom as beasts of burden.

○ European common types – these encompass a whole range of locally named donkeys all of which are small to medium in size, 110–130 cm withers height, and grey to brown in colour. Compared to American and Australian donkeys, European types are small, cobby, compact and stocky. Most have a heavy head, long ears and a broad muzzle and are generally quite willing workers.

○ American common types – these are grey-dun, medium to large animals derived from donkeys imported from Spain in the 16th Century and are often badly kept and in poor condition.

○ Australian common types – these are almost exactly similar to standard and large standard donkeys in America and are strikingly different from imported European types. They are generally 110–142 cm high and quite strong with good bone.

○ Asian common types – found in West India, Sri Lanka, Tibet and Nepal. Some of these are large, up to 112cm high, and used for ploughing while those kept at higher altitudes are stouter and average just 94 cm at the withers. Asian donkeys are usually white or grey and some have zebra-like markings on their legs.

In the developed world donkeys do not just belong to a type, but often to an officially recognised breed. When a new breed is described, an organisation known as the Donkey Breed Society, to be discussed later, produces a studbook to define breed standards and cite the pedigrees of the healthiest thoroughbred animals. The following list gives the breeds of donkey for which such a studbook existed in 1996 (Mason 1996):

○ American Mammoth Jackstock donkey – this is usually black or red, occasionally grey, with white underparts. The breed was developed in America from large donkeys imported from Europe and was once popular with mule breeders. As the mule market declined, however, its numbers dropped and it is now quite rare.

○ Amiatina donkey – this is agouti with a shoulder cross. It originated from Mt Amiata, Grosseto, Italy, but it is now almost extinct.

○ Andalusian donkey – this is grey with noticeably large ears. It was once the most numerous of the Spanish breeds but is now very rare.

○ Asinara donkey – this is small and white in colour. It originated from a tiny island off Sardinia called Asinara and then spread to Sardinia and the Italian mainland. Its numbers were never great and it is now almost extinct.

○ Catalonian donkey – this is a relatively large animal which is black or dark grey with pale underparts. It was once popular amongst breeders of the American Mammoth jackstock donkey but is now very rare.

○ Large Standard or Standard donkey – first described in the USA, this is usually grey-dun and ranges from 36–48 inches high. The breed was developed using particularly large animals bought over to America from Spain in the 16th century and is now very numerous.

○ Majorcan donkey – originating from the Balearic Islands, Spain, this is a local type of the common Spanish donkey which is now nearly extinct.

○ Martina Franca donkey – this is nearly black with light underparts. It originated in Apulia, Italy, but is now nearly extinct.

○ Miniature donkey – this was first described as a breed in the USA and a studbook for it started in 1990. It comes in all the grey, brown and spotted variations of other breeds, but to qualify as a 'miniature' it must be no higher than 36 inches at the withers. Although small, miniatures are well proportioned with long ears, a sloping croup and dainty hooves and are thought to have developed a very long time ago from animals of stunted growth which were the only ones to survive and reproduce in areas with little food. Like stunted forms of other species, these were quite possibly island dwellers and the first registered miniatures were thought to have been bred from Sardinian or Sicilian animals that were imported to America in 1929. Few really small donkeys are still found in the Mediterranean islands and most are kept in America and Canada where they are increasingly popular as pets.

One of the miniature's early advocates was Robert Green, a New York stockbroker who established a donkey stud farm in New Jersey in the 1930s. His enthusiasm for his little animals was summed up in his description of them as possessing 'the affectionate nature of a Newfoundland, the resignation of a cow, the durability of a mule, the courage of a tiger, and an intellectual capability only slightly inferior to man's'. Often called 'minimokes' by newspapers, there are now thousands of miniatures in North America; they are bred both for showing and for keeping as pets, and are promoted by the National Miniature Donkey Association and Miniature Donkey Registry of the United States. About

Willow (an adult
miniature donkey) and
Brittany at Daisydowns
Donkeys Australia

Long-haired donkeys together at the Donkey Sanctuary, Devon, 2004.

8 years ago interest in miniatures took off in the UK and in that time their numbers have risen from about 40 to 400 or 500.

○ Pega donkey – this is large, since the male is 128 cm high and the female, 119 cm, and it is usually roan in colour. It was first described as a breed in Minas Gerais in Brazil and, like other large breeds, it is thought to have been developed using donkeys imported from the Iberian Peninsula.

○ Poitou donkey – so called because it originates from the Poitou region of France, about 300 miles southwest of Paris. It is the largest breed of donkey in the world: the male, called a baudet, has an average withers height of 145–155 cm and a weight of 350 kg while the female, an anesse, is about 10 cm smaller. The Poitou is an unusual looking animal with shaggy or almost curly hair that forms a thick covering on its large ears and a long mane that flicks from side to side. Other distinctive features are its long ears, heavy and bony head, powerful neck, muscular legs and long straight back. Its coat is normally dark brown to black with no clearly definable black stripe and its muzzle, nose and ears are silver-grey.

For hundreds of years the Poitou's sole use was in siring mules and it has thereby made an important contribution to the French agricultural economy and earned itself a worldwide reputation. In its heyday the Poitou was exported to other Mediterranean countries, America, Russia, the Belgian Congo and North Africa but the decline in the mule market meant its numbers declined drastically since the 1950s as some breeders sold or killed their herd. Measures were then taken by the French Agriculture Ministry to preserve the breed and its numbers have now risen from a low point of fewer than 100 to over 400.

○ Ragusan or Sicilian ass – this is particularly large since males are an average 145 cm high, females, 138 cm. It has a nearly black coat and pale muzzle and belly. It originated in Italy where it was used for draught work and mule production, but is now very rare.

○ Zamorano-Leonesa – this has long, black hairy coat with a pale muzzle and underparts. It originated in Zamora and Leon in Spain but is now rare.

CHAPTER 4

The Donkey in Man's World

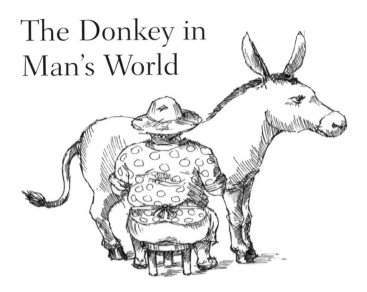

Early History and the Spread of Donkeys around the World

Domestication of animals first occurred around 10–11,000 years ago when humans evolved from being hunter-gatherers who shared their environment with the wildlife to being farmers and stockbreeders who controlled and dominated it. Archaeological remains found around the earliest human settlements reveal that dogs and cats were the first animals to live in close quarters with man. They probably voluntarily joined human encampments after scavenging on left over food. For the next 5,000 years or so cattle, sheep, goats and pigs were all held in captivity to provide a ready supply of food and milk and then it was the turn of horses, camels and wild asses which were mainly used for transport.

As we have already seen, the donkey is the domesticated form of the wild ass. The earliest evidence of its existence consists of ass bones found in an Egyptian Pharaonic burial site known as El Omari which is more than 5000 years old. The first donkeys may well have been kept partly for their milk as in Upper Egypt ancient rock-drawings have been unearthed of tethered animals, presumably in season, calling for the wild ass stallion to visit them.

Since donkeys were domesticated before the invention of the wheel it is presumed that their first main use was as a beast of burden. A pack animal would have certainly been useful to the wandering shepherds and cattlemen in the wild ass's homeland either side of the Nile. Much of ancient Egypt's wealth resulted from trade in precious metals that were carried on the backs of donkeys, as camels were not common until the Graeco-Roman period and Egyptian art of the Fifth Dynasty (2500–2345 BC) frequently depicts asses with saddle cloths and loads strapped to them.

With the discovery of metal working, simple carts, sleds and ploughs were developed but for a long while these were pulled by domestic cattle rather than by horses or donkeys. One of the first pieces of evidence of donkeys pulling carts is the depiction of a battle scene on a wooden box known as the Standard of Ur that dates from around 2500 BC. This was found in Mesopotamia, present-day Iraq, and it clearly shows four-wheeled wagons being drawn by donkeys.

The ancient horse or donkey chariot or cart consisted of a box or basket with two poles and an axle with two wheels. The draught animal was harnessed to the poles by a neck yoke and controlled by means of single reins attached to a noseband. Some of the earliest depictions of donkeys harnessed to carts show four animals side by side with only the central two being yoked and the outsiders attached by reins alone.

The first people to ride equines appear to have been the inhabitants of northern Africa and the steppes of western Asia during the Late Neolithic and Early Bronze eras (3000–2500 BC). The spread of the tradition of riding into Western Europe probably took place alongside parallel innovations of the brewing of alcohol and the emergence of a warrior aristocracy and by 1000 BC horses were a central feature of the rustic economy of prehistoric Europe. In everyday life it was the horse or donkey that pulled the plough and carried the burden and for centuries most riders would have been bareback, as saddles and stirrups were not common until the early Middle Ages.

Pictorial evidence of the riding of donkeys dating from the third millennium shows riders sitting far back on the animal's loins, where its back is flattest. Due to a donkey's low withers and the low carriage of its head and neck, this is the most comfortable position in which to ride it bareback for any length of time and is known as the 'donkey seat'. It is still adopted today by riders in some developing countries. Being positioned so far from the donkey's head, however, means the rider has little control over his mount and is jolted by the shocks of its moving legs. This makes the donkey quite unsuitable for riding at speed and it is unlikely to have ever been used as first choice for hunting or in battle.

Mules

The first people to breed equine hybrids were probably the Sumerians of ancient Mesopotamia, present day Iraq, at the beginning of the third millennium BC. They began by crossing the domestic donkey with the native Asian wild ass but the latter was a notoriously bad tempered animal that was particularly difficult to tame. The wild horse was much better suited to captive breeding and the hybrid between a horse and donkey was a far favourable working animal. Mules, as they were known, soon became essential pack animals all over the ancient world and early Sumerian art shows them being yoked in teams and used to draw war chariots.

Throughout its history, one of the donkey's most important roles has been as sire to what is probably the most useful of all working animals – the mule. A mule is a hybrid produced by crossing a donkey stallion with a female horse and has many of the positive attributes of both its parents. In comparison with the donkey, it has shorter ears, a larger muzzle, a fuller mane, a thinner tail and clumsier hooves. Its voice is half way between that of a donkey and horse, it comes in all sizes from dwarf to giant and its colour can vary from white to almost black – chestnut is very common. Due to a phenomenon known as 'hybrid vigour' a mule is more robust than either of its parents and was recognised from an early stage as being 'everywhere hardier than the horse, subject to fewer diseases, more patient, better adapted to travelling on rugged and trackless surfaces, less fastidious as to its food, and much less expensive in feeding, more muscular in proportion to his weight, and usually living and working to about double the age.' (Warder 1863) At one time mules were so popular that they were divided, in declining order of size, into draft mules, farm mules, sugar mules, cotton mules, and mining mules. The mining mule, a small, rugged individual weighing as little as 600 pounds (270 kilograms), was used in pit mines and was usually produced by pony dams.

For all its uses, however, the mule does have one major handicap – being a hybrid rather than a true species it fails to produce functional gametes and is nearly always sterile. Breeding mules has, therefore, always required a healthy donkey stallion and over the centuries this has benefited many donkeys by ensuring they are well looked after in areas where they may otherwise suffer neglect. Some societies, such as the Jews, however, see the coupling of different species as being contrary to the laws of nature and have always forbidden the breeding of mules. Where this is the case, the donkey was kept on for longer as a working animal in its own right.

Hinnies

While crossing a male donkey with a female horse produces a mule, crossing a female donkey with a male horse results in a hinny or jennet. Theoretically, a hinny has the same characteristics as a mule but as any hybrid animal tends to resemble its mother more closely than its father, hinnies are generally not as strong or robust as mules and have never been very popular. There was once a demand for them in Ireland, however, and in Cyprus they were used for a time as riding animals.

North Africa and Western Asia

It was in the wild ass's native lands of northeast Africa that the donkey was first domesticated, about 5000 years ago. The Ancient Egyptians soon introduced it to western Asia and by 3000 BC donkeys were found throughout present day India, Pakistan and Iraq. Their use as pack animals

Pack donkeys in Afghanistan, ca 2000.

is described in business letters of a group of Assyrian merchants established at the court of a Hittite prince in central Asia Minor in about 2000 BC. These tell of ass convoys regularly crossing the Syrian Desert and the Taurus Mountains in Turkey while an Egyptian relief from Bari Hasan, dating from around 1900 BC, pictures the arrival of the Canaanites with their pack asses laden with children and tribute. Archaeological evidence from all over the Middle East shows that the number of donkeys increased rapidly over the next few hundred years and by 1000 BC they were as common a means of transport in the region as horses were in Europe and the Far East.

In 2006 a complex of tombs was discovered in Syria dating back to the 3rd millenium BC and containing skeletons of infants, decapitated donkeys and puppy bones. The tombs were located near the ancient city of Tuba which was on a vital east-west trade route connecting Mesopotamia with Aleppo and ultimately the Mediterranean Sea. As such it became economically important and with the newly discovered tombs containing signs of the ritual sacrifice of humans and animals, it is likely that they comprised a royal cemetery. Animal sacrifices were a key element of the culture, in that offerings of animals were given to the gods and deceased royal ancestors to eat. The fact that donkeys were found in the tombs hints at their status as one archaeologist comments, 'while modern society might not find as much value in them, donkeys and mules were thought of as royal animals and superior to horses, which were newly domesticated in the days of Tuba. Donkeys still had a lot of cachet and were expensive. I suspect that the sacrifice of these equids [the skeletons were identified as member of the horse family, most likely donkeys, onagers (donkeys' wild cousins) or a hybrid of the two] in our tombs has something to do with their association with the highest rank of society. It would be like a wealthy person today being buried with his or her Rolls Royce.' (Lunday 2006)

References to working asses in the Old Testament hint at the early use of donkeys in the Holy Land. As in the following quotation, 'Moses took his wife and his sons, and set them upon an ass, and he returned to the land of Egypt' (Exodus 4,20)', these commonly describe the ass as being ridden by women and children. Deborah's exhortation to the judges, 'Speak ye that ride on white asses, ye that sit in judgement, and walk by the way' (Judges 5,10) implies that white donkeys were favoured by people at the top of society.

Although the Middle East was the donkey's stronghold right up to the Middle Ages, as elsewhere its numbers declined sharply when domestic horses where introduced. The horse was first thought to have been domesticated around 5000 years ago in the steppe lands of Eastern Asia and then spread very quickly east and west. It did not reach Egypt, however, until about 1675 BC when it was introduced by the Hyksos and it was never a popular working animal there as it was poorly suited to the climate compared to the donkey. Throughout North Africa, the donkey was used by long-distance travellers and small tradesmen and is today still an essential pack animal for people living on marginal desert lands. In urban areas donkeys have largely been replaced by motor vehicles although in Cairo donkey-taxis continue to be used by some tourists seeking a more traditional form of transport.

Donkey as a form of transport in Afghanistan, ca 2000.

China

Today there are about 11 million donkeys in China. This is over a quarter of the total worldwide donkey population and many animals are still heavily used by rural Chinese peasants. Donkeys were first introduced to the region in the 3rd millenium BC by travellers on the Silk Road. This was an extraordinary group of trade routes over 4,000 miles long that wound its way over vast areas of inhospitable terrain from China's Pacific coast, around the northern edge of the Himalayas, through the commercial centres of India and the Near East to the western Mediterranean. For hundreds of years pack animals carried valuable bales of silk and other oriental exotica from east to west along the Silk Road. Each stretch of the way was characterised by the pack animal that was most readily available and best suited to the local conditions. Over the greater part of the journey camels bore the burden but they had their drawbacks: for one thing, horses have an inborn antipathy to camels and camels were somewhat difficult to house at night! Donkeys and mules were better suited to working at high altitudes as they were more sure-footed on the mountainside and could be protected at night by being brought inside or rugged up.

As well as being a popular pack animal, one of the donkey's most important historical roles in China has been to produce mules for the vast armies. The early Chinese military had a variety of roles for their mules: army generals rode them to get a wider field of view over the battleground; standard-bearers to render their flags more conspicuous; and trumpeters and drummers to blast out the Commander's orders more effectively. Very large mules, standing 16 hands (163 cm) at the withers, are still valuable working animals in China today and are bred using Mongolian pony mares.

Donkey operating a stone mill for grinding beans and grain in China ca. 1900. Plate from *Farmers of Forty Centuries* (1911).

The Roman World

As in China, most of the first donkeys in what became known as the Roman World were ex-Silk Road pack animals. Macedonia was the western end of the Silk Road and when they finished their journey many pack donkeys were abandoned there and then adopted by locals. Around the Mediterranean, donkeys were soon found a role in early viticulture. They were well adapted to work on vineyards, being slender and nimble-footed enough to pass down steep and narrow rows of vines and could pull lightweight watering and weeding implements. Donkeys not out in the vineyard could be used to carry panniers of harvested grapes or be made to turn the lever of a wine-press.

Although the Greeks introduced donkeys along with viticulture to some of their early colonies, it was the Romans who helped spread them over a wider area. As legions of Roman foot soldiers invaded Europe they took pack donkeys north over the Alps for the first time and spread them around their expanding Empire. In battle, the Roman army used a type of huge catapult that gave such a powerful kick that they called it an onager, another name for a wild ass. For hundreds of years the vast Roman Empire depended entirely on oxen, donkeys, mules and horses for all land transport and postal services. Whenever donkeys arrived in a new region, the local people wasted little time in putting them to work. The Roman author, Varro, writing in the 1st Century BC, recommended that the young donkey begin work when it was three years old and reported that, '[single asses] are mostly drafted off to the mills or to work on the farms when there is carting to be done, or even to the plough where the soil is light, as in Campania. What herd of asses there are generally belong to traders, such as those who convey, by means of pack-asses, oil, wine, corn, and the like, from the country about Brudisium or Apulia to the sea coast.' (Storr-Best 1912: 195–199)

For long distance haulage the Romans preferred the mule to the donkey. They were certainly good at breeding powerful mules, as they invented a special machine consisting of a sloping wooden cage to enable a jackass to mount the largest and strongest available mare. The Romans also established a system whereby any male donkey foal that was considered a suitable mule sire was removed from its mother and fostered onto a mare. The donkey would then become familiar with the behavioural patterns of a horse and would more readily mount a mare. When a mule was born it was recommended to leave it with its mother for a year and then, 'put to feed far away in the mountains or in wild places so that it may harden its hoofs and presently be fit for long journeys.' (Clutton-Brock 1999)

Britain

Although donkeys probably first came to the British Isles as part of the Roman invasion in about 43 AD, for about 1500 years no one bothered much about them and they were largely confined to the heaths of East Anglia. It was not until the 16th century, when Romany gypsies travelled around the country with their luggage on pack asses, that donkeys spread to other regions. As in other countries where they co-existed with mules and horses, donkeys in Britain were only really ridden by those who could afford nothing else. They played such an insignificant part in British agriculture that they are scarcely mentioned in early veterinary books.

One old agricultural manual that does, however, refer to donkeys is, *The Husbandman's Instructor* written by A. Speed in 1697. This contains a lengthy 'Treatise of Asses, as to their nature, breeding, feeding, ordering and curing the sundry diseases incident to them.' It laments the fact that in England, '*(by reason of the abundance of good horses) riding on him [the ass] is accounted scandalous, and not used, but by the meaner sort*'. Speed argues that if in this country we '*should lay them aside as useless for riding, there is notwithstanding, much business they are capable of: for, as to carrying burthens, the larger sort are comparable to horses; they will hold out a long way without fainting or tireing. Then, for drawing burthens in a cart, they are very serviceable; as also at the plough, in light ground, or where there is no roots of trees, stiff clay, or large stones; for indeed, any creature put beyond its strength, is foiled and disordered, and makes it unpleasant to him for the future.*' (Speed ca.1697:100–103)

Traditional Yorkshire milk boy on donkey. Plate from *Costume of Yorkshire* (1814).

The heyday of the donkey in Britain was in the 19th Century when it was well established as the poor man's workhorse, used to transport anything from bread and milk to firewood, laundry or children. When fitted on each side with basket panniers a sizeable animal could carry one small child in each basket and a third on its back. Small businessmen from cockle-collectors to broom sellers used them for fetching and carrying, and draught donkeys were used to pull anything from rubbish carts for local councils to lawnmowers for wealthy households. In the early coalmining industry, donkeys played a significant role carrying firewood to the furnace and delivering coal direct from the pit head. Where coalmines were some distance from habitation, miners would ride them to work across open moorland. Donkeys have left their mark in the industrial world with 'nodding donkeys' still being used for drudging, repetitive work.

A good example of how donkeys affected life in a rural English community can be found in the village of Chalford in Gloucestershire.

This is spread along one side of a steep mill valley and donkeys were used until the 1950s to carry panniers of bread, milk and wood, etc. around the houses. Well-trodden donkey lanes zig-zagged up the hillside and these remain today as public footpaths. One of the last working donkeys in Chalford was known as Jenny and, in a direct link with the past, one of her descendants still lives as a pet in the village today. In February 2008 a campaign was started by villagers to 'bring back the Chalford Donkey' to partly replace cars ferrying shopping to houses around the steep sided valley. Two donkeys were purchased for the village, one two-year-old and one younger apprentice. The older donkey was trained up with volunteers and started Saturday morning delivery rounds which became increasingly popular – it remains to be seen if this will catch on elsewhere.

Along the valley bottom at Chalford is the remnants of the Thames and Severn Canal, constructed to link a string of industrious woollen mills to the Thames and Severn Estuary. Donkeys were once used instead of horses to pull barges along this and although the canal has now fallen into disuse, the towpath remains, as does an old canal man's cottage which has a converted stable on the bottom floor. The beams in this old stable still bear the original hooks used to hang the barge donkeys' harness and the ghost of a friendly ass is said to haunt the premises.

One Chalford resident, Mabel Smith, who remembers the barge donkeys well, recalls the following:

'I can remember the barges coming up when I was a girl. We used to run down to watch the barges and the poor old donkeys pulling them up the canal. They had donkeys because horses were too big for the towpath. In some parts they used to have to board the donkeys because there wasn't a towpath and the men had to pole the barges. The donkeys knew when they had to stop and they would go no further; they were stubborn as mules! There was always a space left for the two donkeys in the coal barge. They would jump up on to the platform, tearing up there to get into the barge. They knew what to do; they were intelligent.

A 20th-century working donkey in Chalford, Gloucestershire.

The revived working donkey in Chalford, Gloucestershire, 2008.

'Tubby Franklin used to look after the barge donkeys when they came to port. When the barges finished, they took the donkeys up and Tubby had them for good in his meadows. He used to sell those donkeys and he'd say, "If he comes back to me, you can't have him back and you can't have your money back, either." One donkey kept coming back to him – he sold it about six times! In the end, he sold it to someone far away so it couldn't keep coming back.' (Treverton Jones 2004)

Donkeys were not always so popular, however, and in the English village of Broadhempston in the mid 19th century locals complained to the Court of Leet of 'a dangerous and growing evil occasioned by persons permitting their donkeys to stray about the roads, whereby passengers and others on horseback are subject to accidents and serious danger'. They also demanded that donkeys found loose be impounded, and criticised Samuel Tooley, the pigdriver, and the waywardens for 'not attending to the matter'.

In the growing towns and cities of 19th century Britain donkeys were a popular means of transport as they were relatively unflappable and cheap and easy to keep. There were once 100,000 working donkeys in London alone. The London costermonger would not have been complete without his 'moke and barrow' and every Saturday morning about 2,000 of them would flock to the Covent Garden market to load up with vegetables, fish, firewood, etc. As most costermongers lived in the South and East of the city, Smithfield and Borough Markets were also popular. The author of a 19th-century book about London's horses, ponies and donkeys wrote of a moke that, 'like his master he has very strict notions as to what constitutes a day's work, and once he gets home will never go out again if he can help it; and he has a strong objection to working more than six days in a week.'

London's East End People's Palace was once the venue for a triennial Donkey Show and a weekly market held in Kingston, to the west of the city, became the main outlet for the 3,000 or so donkeys sold each year. In the 1890s the average cost of a donkey at market was £2 to £5 while a good pair of carriage horses was worth about £400.

Up until the early 20th century donkeys formed part of London's transport system and even then traffic congestion was a problem as a melee of horses, donkeys, carriages and pedestrians could cause quite a jam. As motor vehicles invaded the city, London's donkeys soon became redundant and by the 1950s none were left – horse-drawn carts struggled on for a few more years but then disappeared as well.

As elsewhere, the demise of the working donkey throughout Britain was brought about by the invention of the combustion engine, though a few eccentrics and wealthy Victorian families kept them on as pets. So severe was the donkey's decline that by the 1930s only about 100 of them were left in Britain and at the outset of the Second World War London Zoo could not find a single entire jack in the whole country. The only known working donkeys in England today are those used to raise water at Carisbrooke Castle on the Isle of Wight, and some that are still fetching and carrying in Clovelly.

In the 1960s, the lack of interest in donkeys was dramatically reversed as the passion for keeping them as pets took off. Parents of the baby boom generation who had a bit of land and leisure time bought them for their small children and many people were tempted to keep a donkey whereas a pony or horse would have been too demanding. In many ways, the donkey soon came to be seen as a more suitable mount for a small child than a pony. The establishment of the first donkey stud in Britain, Ruffs Orchard in Worcestershire, meant that for the first time the donkey was highly regarded in its own right and showing and driving became popular.

The donkey fad of the 1960s developed with even greater fervour into the 1970s and beyond, and the status of the donkey in Britain has now risen from that of an object of ridicule to one almost as elevated as that of the pony. In recent years, the popularity of the films *Shrek* and *Shrek 2* featuring a fast-talking comical donkey have led to a further dramatic rise in the demand for donkeys and many are now being imported into the country. In 2004 The Donkey Sanctuary in Devon that monitors the intake of donkeys at UK ports reported that 'maybe as many as 800 came in last year, when before that it was just a trickle, probably less than ten.' As we have already seen, a donkey makes a good companion for people and for other animals and can live for a long time. Today, it is a common sight in fields around England and southern Scotland and, as in America, miniature breeds are even being kept in back gardens.

Ireland

Much of Ireland is too wet for the donkey to reach its full potential but the absence of long, hard continental winters means donkeys can survive in the drier areas and they have long been a traditional feature of Irish life.

The Roman army introduced the donkey to Britain but they never made it across the Irish Sea and there are no records of the animal in Dark Age or Medieval Ireland. Donkeys are not thought to have arrived in Ireland until the 17th century when they were brought over by army camp followers during the wars between the English and Irish. As armies in those days required a constant supply of horses to serve as battle mounts, there was soon a shortage of horses in Ireland. Local farmers cashed in by selling their horses to the military and re-stocking with donkeys that were cheaper to buy and maintain. As a result, Ireland's donkey population steadily increased and for several hundred years they were an important part of the local rural economy, used to draw potato carts, carry flax for the linen trade or transport milk for dairymen. By the late 19th century over 200,000 donkeys were employed in agriculture alone. They were also worked on the Irish peat bogs and a favoured few carried ladies to take the waters in fashionable spas.

As elsewhere, the donkey in Ireland had its heyday in 19th century and it was then so common that many were exported to England. Their treatment was poor and on arrival in English ports many were in a state of near emaciation and collapse. They were then either loaded into railway cattle trucks or herded to London in droves of up to 100 head. Many donkeys were heavily shod in Ireland and when they reached London their large shoes were removed and light ones fitted. It is said that the often sour-tempered Irish donkeys would not co-operate in the blacksmith's shop and often had to be slung-up for shoeing or put on their backs.

In the 1960s when the demand for pet donkeys in England soared, the Irish once again cashed in. So few donkeys were then left in Britain that they had to be imported from Ireland en masse and were shipped over in loads of 300 at a time.

America

In 1495, the donkey first appeared in the New World as four males and females were brought by Christopher Columbus and used to breed mules which the Conquistadors rode as they explored the Americas. Both donkeys and mules were used to draw covered wagons and carry packs for the early colonists setting out west across the Great Plains towards Oregon. Pack donkeys abandoned by prospectors and travellers survived well as feral animals and soon spread over a large area of the semi-desert North American interior.

The native Amerindian tribes of this continent never took to the donkey on the same scale as they did to the horse and in mountainous regions of Latin America it was the native llamas and alpacas that were the favoured pack animals as they were best adapted to life at high altitudes. Some donkeys, however, did find their way along the steep and rugged mountain passes of the Andes and in such dramatic conditions Low writes that the donkey *'manifests courage, fidelity, and sagacity. He bears his rider along the ledge of the precipice, where the foot can scarcely find a resting-place, and where a false step would entail destruction upon both. Sometimes he descends declivities so steep and dangerous that they seem impassable. The faithful creature stops when he arrives at the edge of the descent, pauses, and will not move until he has prepared himself for the danger. He views the path before him, and at length, bringing his hinder legs beneath him, he glides down the precipice with frightful rapidity. He follows the winding path as if he had fixed in his mind the very track he was to follow. The rider trusts all to his guidance: the slightest check of the rein might disturb the equilibrium, and cause both to be hurled into the abyss below.'* (Low 1845: 437–444)

A donkey taxi in Colorado, 1991.

In the southern states of the US, mules were more useful than donkeys due to their greater heat tolerance and ability to adjust to the prevailing conditions. They were vital to the early economy of the Deep South as the region's large cotton and corn industry would never have existed pre-mechanization without abundant slave labour and working mules. During colonial times mules were not bred in the New World but imported 'ready-made' from England. Once America gained its independence, however, mule breeding started in earnest with the first President, George Washington, requesting some of the largest known donkeys in the world to use as sires. Teams of mules played a vital role in opening up the vast American wastelands as they were used to pull heavy machinery needed in the early construction of roads and railways across the Wild West. They are still used today in the State of Pennsylvania by Amish farmers who shun the internal combustion engine.

The typical American 'donkey' states, in which, historically, donkeys were equally as important as mules, are Texas, New Mexico and Arizona. The place of both animals in US history has been acknowledged in the motto of the American Donkey and Mule Society: 'They Helped Build Our Country' and, as discussed later, the donkey is the symbol of the Democratic Party.

Australia

One of the earliest recordings of the donkey in Australia is contained in a Commissary report, dated 1 July 1794. (Borwick 1981) Up until 1910, donkeys were imported by colonists in small numbers, mainly to the Northern Territory, and used in mule breeding. They were particularly useful in the Victoria River District due to their resistance to the Kimberley horse disease. In the 20th century, however, as elsewhere in the Developed World, the working donkey in Australia was superseded by motorised transport and many were abandoned in the Outback where they reverted to a feral state. By 1920, stock returns from cattle stations (ranches) gave a total donkey population of 655, rising to 909 in 1932. Feral donkeys can be a serious threat to the natural ecosystem and the livelihood of farmers and they thrive so well in the vast desert fringes of Australia that they are continually culled by farmers, conservationists or the pet food industry.

New Zealand is about the only country in the Southern Hemisphere where the donkey has never played a significant role. Unlike Australia where the arid environment favours the donkey over the horse, New Zealand has a wetter climate that makes the horse easier to keep and the donkey has never been much used.

South Africa

The Dutch East India Company introduced donkeys to South Africa in the 17th century where they were used for riding, packing and mule-breeding. Pre-mechanization, donkeys and mules were the most effective form of transport in the Drakensburg Mountains and they were soon put to work in the flourishing Cape vineyards. Both animals were still in demand well into the 20th century and were regularly bought and sold through the *Farmers Weekly* which was available in all British colonies. For example, in February 1937, a farmer from Bloemfontien advertised 'two, young Riding Donkeys (geldings or mares), guaranteed not in foal; comfortable and energetic' while someone from Paardeberg requested a 'donkey jack; must be guaranteed to serve horse mares in veld; not less than 13 hands; black preferred'. (*Farmer's Weekly*, 17 February 1937)

Donkeys thrived in the warm, dry South African climate and feral animals became a major cause of land degradation. Attempts to reduce their numbers have included laws to ban them, taxation and shooting.

CHAPTER 5

Current Use of the Donkey

Donkeys in the Developing World

An estimated 39 million donkeys live in the Developing World (FAO 2005) and the majority are used to transport people and goods, often across difficult terrain where vehicles are unsuitable or unaffordable. For many, a donkey is horse, bicycle and work van combined and in rural areas donkey ownership can aid economic development by enabling people to cultivate their land better and transport crops to market. As working animals, donkeys have the advantages of being drought tolerant, cheap and long-lived when compared to other large domestic animals. They also have a low cull value and so are unlikely to be stolen. Their disadvantages include them having little or no resistance to trypanosomosis, a serious disease in tropical regions, and needing good harnessing and hoof care which can be scarce and expensive. To save money, donkeys in Developing Countries are often fitted with rubber shoes made out of old tyres.

Riding

In many Developing Countries the donkey, due to its small size and placid temperament, is the most suitable mount for women, small children and the sick or disabled. As proper harness is difficult to come by, the rider often sits on a rug, blanket or padded sack placed over the donkey's back. Some animals are ridden without a bit or even a bridle and must be commanded either verbally or with a thin stick directed at the head. People tend to sit either towards the front of the donkey, close to the withers, or on its hindquarters where the back is flattest and women often ride 'side saddle'.

As a general rule, no donkey should not carry more than one-half its own body weight for any length of time, which means an average 130 kg animal should not be burdened with over 65 kg. Those in the Developing Countries are often so underweight that this would exclude almost all adult men and here many carry more weight than they should.

Packing

Again, the rule that donkeys under normal conditions should not carry more than half their own weight applies. In tropical countries, healthy pack donkeys carrying loads of over 50kg can generally travel about 30 km in a day. In practice, though, they are often overloaded and underfed, making them prone to work-related injuries which hinder their progress.

In countries with little motorised transport, pack donkeys often play a major part in restocking local rural communities with food, water, firewood and building materials. Even where motor vehicles are available donkeys can make more efficient transporters in areas with no roads, dense forest, intensively cropped land or very wet ground. In urban areas pack donkeys help out small tradesmen such as builders, potters, tinkers and washermen.

The saddle of a pack donkey is generally known as a 'sunka'. In Developing Countries, this consists of a bolster stuffed with straw and supple sticks or canes that is slung over the animal's back, doubled in the middle and secured with a strap under the belly. The bend of the bolster should be placed well in front of the donkey's withers, so that the animal's spine lies in the space between the double portions. Where possible, the donkey's back should be protected by a thick layer of blankets forming a pad beneath and above the sunka. The weight of the pack needs to be evenly distributed on each side with the load either securely fastened to the frame of the saddle or carried in large baskets, known as panniers, hung over the donkey's back. A donkey travelling up or down hill will need its pack secured at the front by a breast strap and at the back by a breeching strap passed around the hindquarters.

Although most pack donkeys do not travel far out of their immediate locality, some are used for long-distance transport and in northern Ethiopia they are used to carry sacks of salt from the Danakil Depression to Makalle – a distance of over 160 km with an altitude difference of 3,000 m. In the late 19th century, trains of 200–300 pack donkeys transported tobacco from Kano in northern Nigeria some 400 km to the

Donkey ambulance with Sunka in the Imbros Gorge in Crete, 2003.

Current Use of the Donkey | 75

north where it was exchanged for soda (natron). They then took the soda on to Ilorin or Ibadan in southwest Nigeria, a distance of more than 1,000 km, before finally returning home loaded with cola nuts (Ogunremi 1982).

In East Africa most families of Tuareg pastoralists keep 5–10 donkeys and use them to carry essential supplies of water. Donkeys are especially good for this as they drink relatively little themselves. The Tuareg put the water in large rubber inner tubes from lorry tyres and to cut down the amount lost by evaporation these are hung under the donkey's belly rather than slung over its back.

Draught Power

In countries with little mechanisation donkeys are often used as a form of draught power either pulling a cart or plough or pushing against the rotating beam of a static engine. Being relatively small and slim, a donkey can generally manage only about half the draught of a horse and has just a third of the horsepower. A small donkey has about the same draught power as a strong man but a large one can produce over three times the horsepower.

Although most working donkeys are single purpose, they do have a high learning ability and, if necessary, can be taught a wide variety of tasks. They are often used for dull and repetitive tasks such as turning a beam to draw water from a well or rotating a millstone. A single draught donkey can lift an average of 700 litres of water a day through a height of 50 m while a typical 'six-donkey' well can provide sufficient water for either 70 cattle, 140 people or 340 goats or sheep. (Wilson 1990: 581–601)

About 80% of the agricultural draught in the Developing World is animal-driven; oxen, water buffalo, horses and mules are the draught animals of choice but donkeys and camels are used when these are unavailable or unsuitable. Donkeys are used to pull lightweight weeding, sowing and watering machinery; their slender form means they do less damage to crops than heavier animals. They are generally too slight for ploughing, especially in heavy soils.

In Yemen the donkey is the most common draught animal on the 'aqar terraces because it is easier to buy and maintain and far better at negotiating the steep, terraced slopes than its locally available alternative, the bull. In 1978 a donkey or camel could be purchased in the market at Shibam for 1,000 Yemeni riyals – a prime bull would cost 5 to 8 times as much.

In Senegal and Burkina Faso, draught donkeys are used to turn millstones in cereal mills by pushing round a horizontal beam. Flour is the main component of many tropical dishes and traditionally it has been the women's job to produce it. Before animal-powered mills were set up women ground the corn by hand using wooden mortars or stones and once mills were built it became customary for rural women's cooperatives to run them. Donkeys are used for draught power rather than heavier animals such as oxen as it is both easier and more socially acceptable for women to work with them. (Campbell 1990:8-35)

In urban areas of Developing Countries, donkeys can be found pulling carts of anything from refuse to drinks, fish, vegetables and ice creams. They are often used by door-to-door salesmen and in Zimbabwe have even been harnessed to small mobile libraries.

Other Miscellaneous Uses

○ Teaching aids. Being placid and relatively easy to keep means donkeys are sometimes kept at schools where they make good study aids for the children.

○ Smuggling. The donkey's surprising ability to learn and remember a particular route means some have been recruited by smugglers to carry illegal goods through areas where human traffic would arouse suspicion. A donkey is certainly less likely to be stopped and searched than a human and would probably be quite happy to be arrested.

○ Dam construction. In the absence of modern machinery, a donkey's small hard hooves make it an effective force in treading down and compacting earth during pond and dam construction.

Donkeys in the Developed World
On the Beach

In the Developed World many people today associate donkeys with the beach and this indeed is a suitable place for an animal whose wild ancestors roamed the deserts of North Africa. Beach donkeys can work for long hours with relatively little food and water and their small, hard hooves allow them to walk confidently on soft sand.

In Britain, beach donkeys became popular in the 19th century as workers of inland industrial towns flocked to the seaside. In the flourishing Victorian coastal resorts, the donkey provided a chance to ride for people who would never own a horse. Blackpool is a town long associated with beach donkeys and there are currently 228 registered to work on its seafront. A special Blackpool Charter established in Victorian times ruled that the donkeys could not stand in groups of more than 10, had to change stands at regular intervals and should always be kept facing the same direction. Today all British beach donkeys are regulated under the Riding Establishments Act and every year their owners must licence each animal with the local council. To do this they must pay a fee, obtain a veterinary certificate, provide proof of insurance and identify each donkey with either a hoof brand or microchip.

In Autumn 2004 there were 980 licensed donkeys on Britain's beaches and many continue working up until their early twenties. Every August a 'Best Beach Donkey' competition is held and animals are judged on how kind they are to children and how safe parents feel walking beside them. In 2005 Britain's best Beach Donkey was Nosey, from Paignton, Devon, while the Best Group award went to the Nuttall family's donkeys in Skegness, Lincolnshire. (Todd 2006:3)

It is on the Greek island of Santorini that beach donkeys probably have the hardest time. Here they are made to carry tourists up and down steep, winding steps from Ammoudi town harbour to the village of Fira perched on a crater rim above. One such tourist claimed that, 'the Santorini donkeys are matched for cussedness only by those, baleful, spitting, smelly, flea-ridden camels that one finds in front of the Pyramids in Cairo.' (Travelspots 2005) Although a cable car now bears most of the burdens up and down the cliff, when this breaks down or closes for the winter, the local donkeys are brought back into service.

In War

Due to their resilience, relatively unflappable nature and low maintenance requirements, donkeys, and especially mules, have long been used as wartime pack animals transporting baggage, weapons and ammunition over hundreds of miles of rough terrain. It was due to their role as pack carriers for the vast Roman army that donkeys first spread across much of Europe over two thousand years ago and today they are being used to transport explosive devices in the Middle Eastern 'War on Terror'.

Donkeys on Blackpool beach, 1972.

During the Santiago Campaign of 1898, donkeys and mules were the sole means of transportation for the 7th Infantry of the US Army and they were used by British soldiers in parts of India, Sudan, Somalia, Palestine and China right up until the 1930s. Armies on the move would obtain pack mules and donkeys from local people as they were cheap and easy to come by and those bred locally would already be well suited to prevailing conditions. So plentiful were equine pack animals that they were considered highly expendable and about 8,000 horses and mules are thought to have been killed in World War One.

One donkey that played a significant role in the First World War was that belonging to Private John Simpson Kirkpatrick of the 3rd Field Ambulance in the Australian Army Medical Corps. Simpson was a stretcher bearer who became known as the Good Samaritan of Gallipoli when he used his donkey to bring wounded men to the field dressing station at Gallipoli. His donkey, known as Abdul, Murphy or Duffy, had been bought in initially to fetch water and between them they later saved many lives transporting wounded soldiers day and night from the fighting in Monash Valley to the beach on ANZAC Cove. According to CEW Bean, their journey led them through 'deadly sniping down the valley and the most furious shrapnel fire.' Simpson was killed in action aged 22 on 19 May, 1915, having saved the lives of 300 men in the last 24 days of his life. Those who served alongside him said he had escaped death so many times that he became fatalistic and he and his 'little beast earned the admiration of everyone at the upper end of the valley.' What eventually happened to his donkey is unknown but the heroic efforts of both are recounted in one of the most unusual books on equines in war, Benson (1965) *Man with the Donkey*. In Australia, Pte John Simpson Kirkpatrick is viewed as a hero who may well be posthumously awarded the VC whilst in his native Britain there is a statue of him and his donkey in his home town of South Shields on Tyneside. His donkey's role was officially recognised when it was posthumously awarded the Purple Cross – the highest military honour afforded to animals – by the RSPCA in 1997.

According to a manual prepared in the Veterinary Department of the British War Office in 1933, a donkey could carry weights of between 50–150lb although 80lb was the recommended average for military work. Pack donkeys were best travelling in droves and could cover an average of 15 miles a day – they could manage over 20 if allowed to go at their own pace. An animal's rations depended on its size and whether it was on active service – the manual recommended that all donkeys ranging from 9.2 to 10.1 hands high should get 3.5lb grain a day during peacetime and 4lb during war. Further guidelines stated that 'as far as possible males and females should be kept separate owing to their highly developed sexual instincts and trouble caused thereby in camp. Castration may be advisable.' (War Office Veterinary Department 1933)

As already mentioned, today donkeys are heavily involved in the 21st Century 'War on Terrorism'. During the American assault on Baghdad hapless and singed animals were seen pulling carts of rockets through the narrow streets while in Afghanistan they were used to help distribute voting slips for the post-invasion 2004 presidential elections.

A newspaper article on the 2004 Afghani elections described how, in the Hindu Kush mountains, donkeys are still the main beast of burden used to carry polling station equipment and ballot boxes to isolated communities. Some of these communities live at altitudes of up to 3,500 metres and ravines leading to them are so narrow that ballot boxes had to be stacked vertically on the donkeys' backs. It could take them a week to safely deliver their bulky loads. The article stated that 312 of the 'country's humblest beasts of burden' had been loaned by the United Nations at $10 (£5.60) a day. One Afghani, 40-year-old Pir Mohammed, who hired out his animals was a former Mujahidin fighter. He is quoted as saying that, 'donkeys have been the area's only form of transport for as long as I can remember … for 22 years I was in the resistance and we used them for all our supplies. We couldn't have fought the war without them and now we need them for our elections, too. I like them. They're Afghans – treat and feed them right and they go on forever, else die young.' (Lloyd 2004)

Soldiers on donkeys, possibly the Queen's Royal Regiment (West Surrey), 1932.

In a snub to modern technology, the newspaper report contained a dramatic illustration of election officials stranded in the middle of a river with a stalled Russian four-wheel-drive vehicle while a donkey loaded with polling equipment crossed a rickety bridge over their heads. It also described how the Afghans accompanying the donkeys through mountainous central Afghanistan had been equipped with Global Positioning Satellite capabilities so they could give a precise grid reference for the donkeys' progress. 'The Afghans are having some problems with the technology, though. In a test run last week, one reported a grid that placed him in the centre of Tunisia, another claimed to be in the Cook Islands.' (Lloyd 2004)

As Guard Animals

A donkey's tendency to attack animals that it dislikes and bray when alarmed means it can make an effective guard for a farmer's livestock and in parts of Texas, USA, sheep farmers keep donkeys amongst their flocks to protect them from dogs. It has been found that the longer a donkey spends with a flock of sheep the more protective of them it becomes and over 50% of donkeys reared only with sheep will chase away intruders.

Donkey Facilitated Therapy

Donkeys are particularly gentle and affectionate animals that can have a very therapeutic effect on humans. Everyone enjoys spending time with animals that seem to ask for so little and yet give so much in return and the feelings of trust and friendship that a donkey inspires can do much to improve an individual's feeling of self-worth and confidence. The benefits of animal assisted therapy were recognised back in the 18th century when patients of a mental hospice learned self-control through having to care for creatures weaker than themselves and no pet owner would be surprised to learn that merely stroking a cat or dog has been proved to lower blood pressure.

To reap the benefits of donkey facilitated therapy, a specialised unit was set up at the Donkey Sanctuary in Devon in 1999. This arranges for a team of the Sanctuary's most gentle donkeys to travel to residential homes, hospices, etc where people of all ages get great pleasure from spending time with their affectionate visitors. The trips have proved highly popular and beneficial, bringing great enjoyment and comfort to all concerned. More information on the Donkey Sanctuary can be found in a later section of this book.

Donkey Business

The public's enthusiasm for friendly donkeys means a surprising amount of money can be made from loaning them out. Stonehill Donkeys, near Shrewsbury in Shropshire, is one of several organisations that can provide donkeys for events such as donkey derbies, children's parties and county shows all around the country. Occasionally donkeys are hired out to film and theatre companies and some have even gone temporarily to shopping centres and nightclubs. There is also money to be made in selling both donkeys and a vast array of donkey-related products. Top show donkeys in Britain can now fetch anything from £500 to as much as £1,000 and one of the highest prices paid for a single animal was £25,000 – for a racing donkey called Minstrel.

Donkey Products other than Power
Milk
Donkey milk is closer in composition to human milk than that of any other animal. Both milks have a high sugar and low fat content making them very nutritious and, unlike cow's milk, both are albumin milks. Due to the similarity, when a donkey foal is hand-reared it is best given a human milk substitute to drink and man has long used donkey milk as a medicine. It is probable that one of the main reasons for first domesticating the donkey, around 4500 years ago, was to obtain its milk.

For centuries donkey milk has been used to treat the sick and vulnerable and in Paris in the 1880s, donkeys were used for direct suckling at the stable of the Hospice des Enfants Malades. Direct animal suckling was practised in hospitals for syphilitic children, who because of fear of contagion, were never breast-fed. Donkeys, however, were inefficient milk producers because lactation could not be prolonged unless the animals fed their own foals, and the experiment did not last long.

In 19th the century a herd of about 50 jennies, known as milch-asses, was kept in London to provide the City's hospitals with milk. Donkeys were also milked in the streets of wealthy neighbourhoods so parents could buy donkey milk for their children. The yield from one ass was about a quart a day and people could hire an ass in milk for an agreed period at so much per week. The novel, *Donkey Boy*, set in late

19th century England, tells of a young boy who earned the nickname 'Donkey Boy' because his life was saved by ass's milk. (Williamson 1952)

Today, donkey milk is an important part of the diet for remote farming communities in China and Mongolia as well as the Maasi and Turkana pastoralists in Africa. Although no longer drunk in the Western World, it is still recognised as being very nutritious and to dream of drinking donkey milk is said to denote that 'whimsical desires will be gratified, even to the displacement of important duties.' (Parker 2007)

Bathing in donkey's milk is also held by some to have health benefits, a belief arising from the Ancient Egyptian Queen, Cleopatra, who is said to have bathed in ass's milk for one hour to cleanse and enhance her skin. The myth has led to a modern, rather bizarre, trade in donkey milk in America where vendors claim it can soften the skin, improve complexion and 'turn even the most modest, God-fearing gals into sexual wildcats.' (LiveJournal 2007) The milk is actually thought to originate from Iran, Iraq or Libya and then pass into Egypt before being exported to America.

Meat

The consumption of all equine flesh is forbidden in Islam and often considered distasteful in the Western World. In pastoral societies in parts of Africa, China and Mongolia, however, donkey meat is viewed as an important source of protein. In these communities people can be heavily reliant on their live animals and a donkey will only be eaten once it has died naturally.

Today in the Developed World people, often unknowingly, eat donkey meat in salami and feed it to their cats and dogs in the form of pet food with dubious origins. The Italians commonly add it to their sausages and, despite strict animal welfare legislation to prevent it, an underground trade in horse and donkey meat persists in many parts of Europe. Official statistics published by the Food and Agricultural Organisation show that the main European countries trading in horsemeat are Austria, Belgium, France, Italy, Netherlands, Poland and Switzerland. Donkeys entering the meat trade are mainly exported from eastern European countries such as Romania and Bulgaria to Italian or Spanish abattoirs though, as recently as the 1990s, some were found being taken from Ireland, in some instances through UK ports. As one of the major underground trade routes for live donkeys is through Slovenia, the Slovenian Ministry of Agriculture and Veterinary Sciences has been pressurised to monitor the transit of all equids across its borders.

In both horses and donkeys it is the younger and medium-sized animals that are considered to provide the best meat though in France the flesh of the large Poitou donkey is highly valued. In Australia and America some attempt has been made to convert the feral donkey population into pet food although this has so far not proved economically viable.

The following tale indicates that donkey flesh was not a socially acceptable dish in 19th Century western Europe: when the French were in their flight from Spain, after the battle of Vittoria, some stragglers entered a village and demanded rations. The villagers killed a donkey, and served it to their hated foes. Next day they continued their flight, and were waylaid by the villagers, who assaulted them most murderously, jeering them as they did so with the shout, 'Who ate the donkey?'

Blood

In the folk medicine of northern Europe the blood of a donkey was once used as a cure for jaundice. Today the Turkana people of northern Kenya occasionally drink it to supplement their diet.

Skin

Donkey skin gelatin is used as an ingredient in traditional Chinese medicine with donkey skin glue being used in the treatment of menopausal syndrome. The vast majority of the components of Chinese medicines are plant based and donkey skin is one of only a select few animal products used – others include snake powder, deer tail and frog fat. (Worldlink 2007)

In Kenya, the Turkana pastoralists, already reliant on donkeys for milk, meat and, occasionally, blood, have found that the toughness and water resistant qualities of donkey skin makes it good roofing material for their wooden framed houses. In the western world donkey hide was once used to produce shagreen leather and to cover drums played in wartime. Regarding the latter, Robert Louis Stevenson writes in *An Inland Voyage* (1878), 'As if this long-suffering animal's hide had not been sufficiently belaboured during life, now by Lyonnese costermongers, now by presumptuous Hebrew prophets, it must be stripped from his poor hinder quarters after death, stretched on a drum, and beaten night after night round the streets of every garrison town in Europe.'

'Who stole the donkey?' was for many years a jeer against policemen as it was said that when the force was first established, a donkey was stolen and the police became a laughing stock when they failed to discover the thief. The customary response was, 'The man with the white hat' – the reason being that white hats were supposedly made of the skins of donkeys and donkeys were sometimes stolen to be sold to hatters. (Ayto (ed.) 2005)

Hair and Tail

According to north European medieval medicine practiced by the monks who first brought donkeys and Christianity to Europe, the hair and tail of a donkey could be used to combat whooping cough or scorpion stings. It was also believed that the hair cut from the cross on a donkey's back and hung from a child's neck in a bag would prevent fits and convulsions.

Hoof

Again according to ancient north European folklore, gout could be treated by tying the right hoof of a donkey to the left leg of the patient, and vice versa.

Carcasses

In the 18th and 19th centuries dead horses were of some value as they could be sold to meat markets. Donkey carcasses were much tougher and less desirable although some were used on veterinary college dissecting tables.

Manure

Due to the coarse nature of a donkey's diet, its manure is relatively fibrous compared to that of other large herbivores and so makes poor fertiliser, although some isolated communities have no alternative but to use it. In the Developing World, donkey manure is sometimes used as a binder in bricks made from soil and as fuel and in the folklore of northern Europe 'wise women' are said to have prescribed a poultice of ass-dung for 'dimness of the eyes'.

CHAPTER 6

Donkey Ownership and Management

Buying

Before buying a donkey it is important first to consider why it is wanted as this will determine what type of animal to look for – it is not advisable to get a stallion as these are very unpredictable. If a donkey is to be ridden it should be no more than 20 years old, but if it is just to be kept as a pet it may be better to get an older animal – remember, donkeys can live to 50. As they form life-long friendships, donkeys like to have a companion and it is therefore kinder, where possible, to get a pair of them that are roughly the same age. It is, of course, important that owner and donkey like each other so character should be taken into account when selecting an animal. Some authorities have noted the following distinct types of donkey personality: nervous and active; pushy; timid; spoiled; sullen; friendly and trusting; sluggish; ouchy. These characters come in many combinations but there is usually one that will dominate the rest.

In Britain a donkey can cost anything from £50 to £500 depending on pedigree, age and size and maintenance may cost between £300–£500 a year. Miniature or unusually coloured donkeys are the most expensive and the cost of a miniature show donkey that is stud book registered can be £2,000 for a 6 month filly foal, or £1,000 for a colt. Donkeys may be bought through private sale, a market or from an organisation such as the Donkey Sanctuary in Devon (for details, see later) but it is recommended that a foal should be purchased direct from the breeder as its dam can then be checked for any obvious body faults. The vendor should always supply the buyer with a veterinary certificate to prove their animal is in good health.

For the superstitious it is said that to dream of coming into possession of a donkey by present, or buying, means you will attain to enviable heights in the business or social world, and if single, will contract a congenial marriage. (Parker 2007)

Introduction to a New Home

When a donkey first arrives at its new home it is advisable, before releasing it into the field, to let it get to know any other animals over the fence. Donkeys have a hierarchical system and who is the boss has to be sorted out before they can settle down. An owner should watch them during the meeting period to see whether they get on with each other and keep small pets such as dogs, cats or geese well out of the way.

In most cases new arrivals should settle in well and could even bring benefits; seeing in your dreams a strange donkey among your stock, or on your premises, is taken to signify that you will inherit some valuable effects. (Parker 2007)

Naming

When it comes to naming, certain rules do apply if you intend registering a donkey with the Donkey Breed Society (DBS). The DBS is a British charity that provides support and advice for all donkey owners and will be described in more detail under the section on Donkey Breeding. The organisation strongly recommends that, '*a name is not misleading, distasteful or uses a prefix/suffix incorrectly'* and give 'Smokey' or 'Bramble' as suitable examples. To be accepted for registration by the DBS, the name must not be more than 25 characters long, including any spaces, and once officially recorded it cannot be changed in any way.

The DBS rules, which can appear fairly complex, mean that once a name has been registered with them and the appropriate fee paid, the owner is granted sole rights to that name across all member societies. Suffixes/prefixes can be added to a donkey's name but these will need to be registered separately and another payment made. In the DBS's own words, *'if you registered the name 'Superdonks' with the CPR [Central Prefix Register], no-one else could use this name ... You would only be allowed to use it within the DBS, unless you paid a secondary fee to any other society, in which case you would be able to use it with them also (e.g. you could also breed 'Superdonks' Arabs if you registered 'Superdonks' with them also)'* (Donkey Breed Society 2007) To clear up any misunderstandings regarding the naming process, the DBS is a member of the Central Prefix Register and employs a registrar who can be contacted for advice.

To help in tracing bloodlines, the DBS rules that, *'where you have bred the animal (i.e. owned or leased the mare at time of foaling) you MUST use the prefix for any foal e.g. ' "Superdonk Fluffy"'.'* (In this example the mare would have been called Superdonk). In the case of a donkey not being registered with the DBS, *'you can choose whether to register the animal with or without your suffix, e.g. just as "Blackie" or as "Blackie of Superdonks".'* (Donkey Breed Society 2007)

Licensing

Owning a donkey in Britain today is not as hassle-free as it may at first appear. Since 30th June 2004 every horse, pony, donkey, mule and hinny throughout the European Union must by law have its own individual passport before it can be bought, sold or transported to any new area. The '2003 Horse Passports Order in England', which applies to all equines, contains no fewer than 25 regulations and to give some idea of its style, one rule states that an animal's passport must 'be obtained by 31 December in year of birth, or six months after birth – which ever is longer – or before then if leaves for a period of more than 2 weeks the premises on which its dam is normally kept' (DEFRA 2003) The passport application form runs to approximately eight A4 pages.

The primary reason behind the horse and donkey passport system is not so much to benefit animals as to safeguard public health by ensuring that animals treated with certain medicines do not enter the food chain. To this end it must record what veterinary treatment the donkey receives and state whether or not it is intended for human consumption. To help match donkey to passport, the application form must describe as fully as possible any of the animal's distinguishing body markings.

In England there are currently over 70 organisations authorised to issue passports and, as these can charge what they like for doing so, it pays to shop around. Local authorities are responsible for enforcing the legislation and any owner not complying with it can face a fine of up to £5,000 or three months imprisonment.

Housing

A donkey kept outdoors should have no less than half an acre of grass or it may run out of food. A good way to ensure a constant supply of fresh grass is to divide a donkey's field in two and then rotate the grazing so that one half is always resting. Donkeys are selective grazers so careful pasture management is important and as well as good grass, a field needs a fresh water supply and should be free of poisonous plants such as ragwort, privet, bracken, yew, rhododendron, deadly nightshade, box, mare's tail, laburnum or lupin. Whenever they can, most donkeys like to eat bark and wood so any trees, or even fencing posts, within reach should be well protected. Pieces of wood left lying around the field make good toys for donkeys and a patch of coarse sand that they can use as a rolling spot will be appreciated.

Donkeys will happily eat coarse, unpalatable plant matter such as thistles, brambles and even cacti – some actually seem to choose this over succulent pasture. Such dietary preferences mean donkeys can quite happily share a field with other grazers as they won't always be competing for the best grass. Mixed grazing with sheep works well as these will eat the grass down tight and so reduce the amount of parasitic worms in a field. Another way of keeping down the worm population is to regularly remove any dung.

A donkey must always have access to a fresh supply of water. It generally drinks from 4–8 gallons a day and may need more in hot and arid environments. (The Royal Veterinary College 1991:6–11) When horses and mules went to war it was found that they could survive without food much longer than they could without water. Donkeys are more efficient than horses at conserving water, a trait they have inherited from their desert dwelling ancestors, and if dehydrated can rapidly replenish themselves.

A donkey's field needs to be well fenced or hedged. Field boundaries can be lower than those of a horse's enclosure but in order to be donkey-proof they do need to be robust – a donkey can squeeze out through a narrower gap than a horse can and may even eat its way through a hawthorn or bramble hedge. If it does escape it will tend to just wander a short distance and pick at things while looking around. A placid donkey can be tethered to graze but this should not be done for long periods and

Donkey grazing.

the tether should be moved regularly. Some owners may loan their donkey to a neighbour who can tether it and use it to eat down any unwanted long grass or roughage.

As well as an outdoor area, a donkey needs access to a stable or shed in which it can keep warm and dry and get away from flies. A donkey left out for too long in heavy rain or a cold wind can quite easily catch pneumonia, as although its coat is long it contains few protective oils. Any form of shelter should be at least 32^2 ft (72 ft^2 for two) and should be well ventilated, have a hard, level floor and not too many windows as these encourage flies. (The Donkey Sanctuary 1992) A donkey is not fussy about its accommodation and has been known to live happily in a garage or a sun loggia attached to a small house, though if kept in too long it may become bored and a distraction such as a piece of wood it can chew on will help.

All indoor donkey enclosures should be provided with a bedding of clean, dry straw. Any surplus can be piled up along the wall to act as a cushion. Straw is also an important source of roughage for a donkey and some may eat their bedding. This habit has given rise to the old English phrase, 'a donkey's breakfast', which refers to a sailor's mattress filled with straw.

Security

Because donkeys are often left alone for long periods they are prone to being lost, stolen, or, in remote areas of some countries, eaten by predators. To stop a donkey escaping or being got at, it is therefore important to keep all field gates and stable doors securely fastened. Many owners like to keep their donkeys close to their house as this makes the donkey easier to watch. In Britain, most reported donkey theft has occurred in the Home Counties and some local Horsewatch groups have been set up there. The incentive for stealing a donkey appears to be the increasing value of some thoroughbreds, though there must be easier ways of making money.

Feeding

The average donkey needs about ¾ of the amount of food required by a horse. As with all animals, the amount and type of food an individual

needs depends on its condition and how hard it works – mothers that are lactating and donkeys that are still growing should have the most. Most donkeys, whether working or idle can survive solely on grass, approximately 1.25 m^2 per donkey per day (The Royal Veterinary College 1991:6–11) but old and sick animals may need 'feeding up' in winter with supplementary foods such as bran or concentrated foodstuffs such as horse nuts. A donkey kept indoors will need a daily supplement of minerals and vitamins and supply of fresh hay. To prevent overfeeding, hay should not be fed on an ad-lib basis and one bale every 5 days should suffice.

Some of the donkey's favourite supplementary foods are kitchen scraps such as vegetable peelings and stalks. Carrots, turnips, swedes, cabbages, cauliflowers and apples can all be given as a treat but should be cut up into pieces to prevent a donkey choking. Bread is also popular, though this is fattening and more than a slice a day can cause stomach ache. Two foodstuffs to avoid are grass cuttings and large quantities of feed designed for other animals as these can be too rich. All donkeys appear to have a sweet tooth and will find ginger biscuits, sugar lumps and mints very tasty.

As described earlier, the donkey has a remarkably efficient digestive system that is capable of turning the plainest of foods into pure fat. Many donkeys left in a field of rich grass, though very content, can become so overweight that they are at risk from a condition known as hyperlipaemia. This occurs when a donkey with too much excess fat becomes stressed. Stress can mobilize surplus fat into the bloodstream where it adversely affects the kidneys and other organs and, in extreme cases, the condition may be fatal. Donkeys that become obese can also suffer a very painful and stressful disease known as laminitis in which an increased strength in its digital pulse causes an animal to stand on its heels for relief. Again, this can lead to death and if it is suspected, a vet should be called.

In an age when donkeys were more often used as working animals, it was important to keep them well fed through the winter months. The following advice on 'how to order the ass in snowy, or hard frosty weather, when there is little to be got abroad' is taken from 'The Husbandman's Instructor' written in 1697. '*In the winter season, if the snow be on the ground especially, you must feed him in the house with chaff; sweet pease-straw, and hay chopped short; hard bisket, or chipings of coarse bread beaten small; and to comfort and keep them in heart, fit for service, give them now and then bran is sweet shey, skim-milk or wort; but it must be very thick, or [...] he will hardly wish for it, though never so hungry.*' (Speed 1697:112–117)

Medication

Donkeys are relatively robust and disease-resistant and can usually survive with less attention than horses. In the Developed World, their greatest health problems are probably pneumonia, laminitis or stomach upsets bought on by lack of shelter, over-consumption or eating the wrong type of food. In developing countries, donkeys are most at risk either from malnutrition or from injury resulting from ill-fitting harness or mistreatment at work and these can usually be cured by normal methods. One thing the domestic donkey has inherited from its desert dwelling wild ancestors is immunity to diseases commonly found in hot and arid environments. In Australia it does not succumb to Kimberley horse disease and in Africa it is only rarely affected by African horse sickness.

When compared with horses, donkeys show fewer overt signs of pain such as fretting and rolling and when suffering tend just to lie down or stand with their heads lowered. Early indications of ill health are seeing a donkey standing on its own or in an unusual stance with its ears back. It may also appear lethargic and have a general lack of interest in its surroundings. Even donkeys with severe abdominal pain rarely lie down and roll but instead have little appetite, a mildly elevated heart rate and a vague reluctance to move – not easy signs to detect. (McGreevy 2004)

A couple of basic health checks owners can carry out are taking their animal's temperature and pulse rate. A donkey should never be regarded as a small horse for medical reasons as its normal body temperature is slightly lower than that of a horse; 98.8°F (37.1°C) compared with 100–101°F (37.8–38.3 °C). Its temperature is taken by inserting a thermometer into the rectum where it should be held for a few moments before the reading is taken. Its pulse rate can be checked by gently placing the ball of a finger on an artery located under the donkey's lower jaw where a slow throbbing should be detected. A young donkey's pulse may vary between 36–80 beats a minute with a median value of 44 for a resting animal.

Some of the more common causes of disease in donkeys in any area and the symptoms, treatment and methods of prevention of various ailments are described below:

○ Internal parasitic diseases. Probably the most frequent health problems in donkeys are caused by infection with internal parasites such as ascarid worms, large and small strongyle worms, flat worms, lungworms and liver flukes. All donkeys carry a mixture of these in some part of their stomach, intestines, lungs and liver but in most cases they can survive perfectly well as there is plenty of food in their gut to go round. If an animal is underfed or weakened, however, its internal parasites may multiply to a point at which they extract too many nutrients from their host. This can result in the donkey becoming slow, lethargic and quickly fatigued which may make it more susceptible to other diseases such as pneumonia. Signs of a serious worm infection include a staring coat, large belly, visible ribs and segments of worm in the stool. If heavily infected with strongyle worms, the arteries of a donkey's small intestine can become blocked and this may be fatal.

To stop internal parasites building up in their gut, all donkeys should be regularly treated with wormers or anthelmintics. Regularly removing dung and keeping the grass in a field short will also help reduce the amount of internal parasites since old, long grass harbours more of their eggs and larvae.

○ External parasites. These include lice and mites which live on the donkey's skin and can cause patchy hair loss resulting in a condition known as mange. Further symptoms of skin infections are excessive rolling on the ground, rubbing, scratching and biting at the skin. Prevention measures include giving a donkey enough food, keeping its bedding and harness clean and brushing its coat to get rid of any parasitic eggs. Special chemicals deter lice and mites and these can be applied as dips, sprays, powders or pour-ons.

Ticks are large, blood-sucking insects that attach themselves to the soft skin either under a donkey's tail, on the inside of its upper legs or in its ears. They can transmit disease-causing blood parasites and, in large numbers, may lead to a significant loss of blood. They can usually be picked off by hand and destroyed by crushing underfoot but where necessary can be treated with the chemical, acaricide, which will cause them to drop off after a few hours.

○ Fungal infections. Diseases caused by fungi are not usually life threatening but are contagious and should be treated with anti-fungal cream. Ringworm is one fungal infection that causes small, hairless circles, nodules and abscesses to appear on the skin. Epizootic lymphrangitis is another and results in lumps under the skin which discharge a thick yellow pus. The lumps can sometimes occur in a donkey's eyes where discharges may build up on the facial hair and attract flies. Recovery from both infections often occurs unaided but treatment involving surgical removal of nodules is available. Prevention measures for all diseases spread by fungi include the isolation of infected animals and the regular cleaning and disinfection of items such as harness and rugs which can harbour fungal spores.

○ Bacterial diseases. Various types of bacteria can cause anthrax, glanders, tetanus and dermatophilosis, all of which are rare in Britain but can be a serious problem in Developing Countries.

Anthrax is characterized by high fever, depression, difficulty in breathing and bleeding and may be transmitted to humans if they eat or touch the corpse of an infected animal. The condition is often fatal though if discovered early enough it can be treated with penicillin.

Glanders is another contagious and often fatal bacterial disease in which swelling glands just under the skin or in the respiratory tract result in ulcerating nodules and coughing. It can be treated with antibiotics but these are often ineffective and any infected animals should be immediately destroyed.

Tetanus, sometimes called lockjaw, is caused by a poisonous toxin produced by a bacterium which makes the whole donkey become stiff and often unable to open its mouth. A diseased animal deteriorates quickly and there is no effective treatment. Prevention comes in the form of a vaccine that is relatively cheap and widely available in the Developed World.

Dermatophilosis results from a bacterium getting into the skin via an injury or insect bite. It is the donkey equivalent of dermatitis in humans and is characterised by matted hair and the formation of scabs and cuts. It can be treated with antibiotics, ointments and tick control regimes.

○ Protozoan Diseases. These are collectively known as trypanosomosis, a condition caused by microscopic blood parasites known as trypanosomes. As trypanosomes are transmitted by tsetse flies, the disease is found only in the tropics where it can result in recurrent fever, progressive weight loss and anaemia. Although drugs are available these are hard to come by in Developing Countries and the best prevention measure is to destroy the tsetse flies by extensive bush clearing. (MacDonald & Low 1985:62–66)

○ Viral Diseases. The two main equine diseases caused by a virus are African horse sickness and rabies. The former occurs only in sub-Saharan Africa and is characterized by fever, rapid breathing and coughing. It rarely affects donkeys, however, as most inherit immunity to it from the wild ass. Rabies is again restricted to the Developing World due to a readily available vaccine elsewhere. Animals with the disease may become either unusually dumb or seemingly mad and rabid donkeys tend to bray continually and run around champing their jaws. Rabies is always fatal and, as it is most commonly spread by the bite of an infected dog or fox, the best way of preventing it is to vaccinate all dogs in an area. (MacDonald & Low 1985:62–66)

In an age before conventional veterinary medicine, donkey owners often had to diagnose a donkey's ailments and gather and dispense treatments themselves. An early veterinary textbook, *The Husbandman's Instructor* produced in 1697 contains the following section on donkeys headed, 'Diseases particularly incident to them; and their cures'.

Pains in the Head

This comes from wet and cold in travel or lying; and sometimes of extream heat in the hot summer season. To remedy this, take Polipodium of the oak, a handful; wood-sorrel, or field-sorrel, a like quantity; boil them in stale beer, and give it him hot; soon after let him blood behind the ears.

For Defects in the Lungs

This is known by his heavy and painful breathing, his lamentable braying, not clear, but inwardly as it were. To remedy this defect, boil liquorish well bruised two ounces; century a little handful, in three pints of running water, till a third part be consumed; then give it him at two equal potions well strained, morning and evening fasting.

For the Hide-bound

This is occasioned by being too much in the wet and cold; To remedy it:

Let him blood under the tail; rub him well over with hard wisps; boil the roots of fennel in new wort, a handful to a quart; add an ounce of lupius, and half as many camomile-flowers; give it as a drench, a pint at a time, morning and evening.

To purge Melancholy

Take three or four laurel-leaves, a sprig or two of savin, a quarter of an ounce of stibium, boil them, well bruised in a quart of whey, and give him the liquid part well strained, to drink, and let him fast six hours after.

For Madness or Giddiness

This is occasioned by the contending of heat and cold in the brain; from vapour arising by bad digestion. To remedy it:

Take a handful of the tops of rue and cardus, boil them in a pint of white-wine; and just before you give it him, bleed in the Temple-Veins. Tie him up close in an airy place, for six hours; then give him water wherein wild cucumber-roots have been boiled, and good litter.

To prevent Diseases

Pick his feet clean from gravel and dirt; wash them with warm chamberly, and stop them with goats or beef suet; over that flax, dipped in tar; give him in a pint of ale, an ounce of methridate, and a quartem of olive oil.

For swellings, sores, bruises, broken bones, sprains and the like, do as in care of bullocks, sheep, etc.' (Speed 1697:112–117)

Pedicure

The hooves of a donkey that, unlike its wild ancestor, does not travel long distances over rough terrain will grow very quickly and, if not cut regularly, can become cracked and infected resulting in lameness. Most donkeys will need their hooves trimming every 6–8 weeks and this should always be done by an experienced farrier. When the blacksmith arrives an owner should have their donkey ready and waiting as if he has to first catch the donkey this will waste his time and increase costs.

It is only necessary to put shoes on a donkey if it is kept on stony ground or tarmac. Shoes are made of metal and should not be too heavy for the donkey's slender legs. The donkey's tender soles can be punctuated by stones and other sharp objects that become lodged inside its hooves, so these should be regularly picked out. Owners can inspect and pick out their donkey's hooves themselves and a final application of hoof oil will make a donkey look really smart.

The advice for basic hoof-care in afore-mentioned *The Husbandman's Instructor* of 1697 was, *'if their hoofs grow out of shape; pare them, and bring them into a fashionable form, that they may grow in thickness; in many places where they labour much, or go on stony ground, they are shooed; but this must be done lightly, and within compass, that they interfere not, to lame them in their treading'.* (Speed 1697:112–117)

Grooming

All donkeys really enjoy being groomed and as mutual grooming between two animals is a way of showing their appreciation for each other, grooming by an owner will help strengthen the bond between them and their donkey. Grooming also has a massage effect on a donkey helping to calm it down and improve its circulation. It will improve the condition of a donkey's coat freeing it of caked dirt and sweat marks but care should be taken not to over-brush, especially in winter, as this may destroy the animal's natural protection.

When grooming, all brush strokes should follow the direction of hair growth and the appropriate type of brush should be used on different parts of the body. A soft body brush is needed for the sensitive face, legs and belly while a rubber or metal currycomb or stiff-bristled dandy brush is better on the mane and tail. Strong brushstrokes with a currycomb will help remove loose hairs when a donkey is moulting and the tail should not be allowed to get matted and dirty.

Training and Disciplining

The best way to catch a donkey is to approach it slowly with an offering of food although an animal that recognises its owner's voice will sometimes come when called. A donkey should always be approached from the front as it dislikes being taken unawares. If it does become evasive it should be cornered into an area from where it cannot easily escape. To make catching an animal easier, it should be caught regularly and not just for unwelcome reasons, such as the blacksmith or vet.

To aid its future relations with humans, a donkey should become accustomed to being handled from as young as possible. Within a few months of birth a foal should be called by its name, get used to being touched on any part of its body and allow itself to be led by a halter or

neckband. It should then be trained
to have its hooves picked up and
examined and to eat concentrates
from a bucket. Having things
placed on its head and back will
prepare it for being broken in at
a later stage.

Breaking in an animal
means getting it used
being harnessed and ridden.
A donkey can be harnessed at about one year old but should not be ridden
until it is four and its skeleton has properly developed. Most animals very
soon learn to accept a head collar and saddle and will readily take to a bit
if it is covered with honey. Compared to a horse, a donkey will make little
fuss when a saddle is first placed on its back and will quickly allow a rider
to mount.

Training a donkey for light work is best carried out before it is 2½ years
old and becomes moody and truculent, but training for heavy work should
be left until it is at least 3. Lessons should begin with a donkey being
fitted with a head collar and led on short walks up and down a quiet lane.
It should always be led from the left as this is the conventional side
for controlling equids. The next step is to teach it to respond to the
standard prompts of 'walk on', 'halt' and 'trot on'. Trainers may reward
good behaviour with food, verbal encouragement or a gentle pat on the
neck although food should not be offered too often as this can encourage
an animal to nip. Another treat is a gentle scratching of the inside of the
donkey's ears – this is one of its chief pleasures causing it to stretch its
neck and half close its eyes.

The best ways to punish a badly behaved donkey are to tap it lightly
at the top of its forelegs, tuck its head under an arm, pinch a fold of
loose skin over its shoulder or, in extreme cases, hold its ear. A donkey
mare will scold her foal by nipping it across the top of the front legs,
just below the chest.

A donkey's lessons should be kept short and varied as, being a relatively intelligent animal, it learns quickly and tends to become bored and badly behaved in long, repetitive training sessions. Another tip is to keep a donkey indoors in between lessons as a stabled animal appears to look forward to and co-operate more in its lessons than one living in a field.

Some of the earliest known advice on 'the ordering and weaning the ass-colt; when to break him' was contained in *The Husbandman's Instructor*. This recommended that, *'the ass-colt when cast, suffer it the first year to run with the dam, and the next, tie him up gently with her, only in the night time: the third is a fit season to break him, and render him tractable for labour, which will not be very difficult to do, by reason of his innate dullness and easiness to be handled.'* (Speed 1697:112–117)

'As with all individuals, some donkeys and people 'get on' while others just don't and if, after a trial period, the two remain at odds it may be best to give up on training altogether. Don't be too disappointed if this happens as it has long been recognised that it is not easy to control a donkey – to dream of leading an ass by a halter is said to show you will be master of every situation, and lead women into your way of seeing things by flattery.' (Parker 2007)

Transportation

Today there are rules in place for numerous aspects of animal welfare from abandonment to zootechnics. Current legislation for the transportation of animals is included in the 'Welfare of Animals (Transport) Order 1997' which contains sections on the following: vehicles, trailers and equipment used; loading density and headroom; space requirements; segregation; loading and unloading; holding facilities; documentation to accompany animals in transit; provision of feed, water and rest. The following two paragraphs are taken from the above Act and serve to illustrate the complexity of the regulations now in place:

> *It is preferable for horses to be transported in individual stalls which are designed to protect the animals against jolts. However, horses may be transported in groups providing that their hind hoofs are unshod, animals*

which are hostile to one another are not transported in the same group and there is sufficient floor space to ensure that they are not crowded in a way that is likely to cause injury or discomfort'

'Unregistered horses, including foals, may not travel more than 8 hours in a basic grade vehicle, after which they must be unloaded and rested for 24 hours and given food and liquid for 24 hours before continuing their journey. In higher grade vehicles, adult unregistered horses may travel up to 24 hours before a 24 hour rest is required, which, if on an intra-Community journey, must be at an approved EU staging point.' (MAFF 1997)

Strictly speaking, the 'Welfare of Animals (Transport) Order 1997' applies only if the transportation is of a commercial nature, i.e. if the animals concerned are kept for profit, but it is generally expected that all pet owners maintain welfare standards at least equivalent to or higher than the legislation.

Animal transportation has not always been so highly regulated, however, and *The Book of the Donkey* written by Robin Borwick, the first Chairman of the Donkey Breed Society, and published in 1981 refers to a time when things were somewhat more relaxed. This contains the following advice: *'donkeys – particularly single donkeys – usually travel much better if they are loose. Most like to put their bottoms in one corner, knowing that they will then easily absorb any shocks';* *'a donkey's hindquarters are quite light, and while you are leading the front end a man may easily lift the hindquarters off the ground completely (if the coat is furry enough to grip) and gently force him in, trundling him like a wheelbarrow'; 'donkeys do not like travelling sideways, and the space may be minimal, but it can be done if you drive as steadily as possible ... the more confined the animals, the less chance of them bumping about.'*

As a donkey owner himself, Robin Borwick certainly seemed to find that transport presented few problems as *The Donkey Owner's Guide* written in 1970 by R.S. Summerhays, former President of the Donkey Breed Society, contains a photograph of him departing from a show with a small donkey lying on the passenger seat of his car.

Another book, this time a novel based on an amateur donkey owner's experiences in the 1960s, describes how a donkey mare in foal bought at a market was, at the suggestion of the vendor, transported to her new home in the back of a Land Rover. Although her buyers were at first hesitant they soon found the donkey was as 'quiet as an old sheep dog' and was easily got into the back of their vehicle. 'Half an hour later we were racing along the Redruth by-pass with me at the wheel, Jeannie beside me, and between the two of us, shoulder level, the solemn, patient face of Penny the donkey.' Tangye (1965: 33)

On arriving at the end of their journey, the new donkey owners found that, as it was wet outside, Penny was not as keen to get out of the Land Rover as she had been on getting in:

'Unfortunately her bottom faced the wrong way. 'Come on, Penny,' I said, gently pulling the rope of the halter, 'turn round.' She stayed staring across the front seats at the windscreen. ...I pulled again, firmly this time. It was like pulling a tree trunk.'

[When a carrot was offered to Penny as an enticement to exit the vehicle] 'she did a neat turn. The well of the Land Rover is only four feet by three, a small space for a donkey in foal, but she manoeuvred herself with the ease of a large dog. Her bottom to the driving seat, her face thrust forward, peering into the rain and growing darkness, she now expected her reward.'

[Further tempting with the carrot meant that, eventually,] 'she [Penny] did not jump, she scrambled; and in one awful moment three of her legs were on the ground while the other was left sprawling in the Land Rover. ... Penny, realising her predicament, paused a few seconds to gain balance on the three legs already on the ground, then leapt forward bringing the fourth one clear. 'Our first lesson,' I said, mockingly serious, 'let her look after herself.' (Tangye 1965: 45–48)

Breeding

For hundreds of years the breeding of donkeys in Britain was a haphazard and unregulated activity. Little care was taken to pick the best animals to breed from with the result that most of the donkey population was of poor quality and considered 'scrub-type'. The problem was addressed in the 1960s when the first donkey stud in Britain, Ruffs Orchard in Worcestershire, was set up by Robin Borwick and selective breeding programmes introduced to produce the best possible donkeys for riding, driving and showing.

In 1968, following the success of his stud, Robin Borwick founded the Donkey Breed Society (DBS). This established guidelines for distinguishing between different 'breeds' of donkeys and in 1969 published a donkey Stud Book to officially register both stallions and mares that were considered the best breeding stock. The Stud Book has since been regularly updated and in order to gain entry all donkeys have to pass a strict inspection process and be certified free of any hereditary disease. Standards for inclusion have always been high and the following faults will all count against an applicant: knees or feet turned in or out, hind legs that were sickle-shaped and cow-hocked, a narrow chest, an over-heavy head, a short neck and a mean croup and quarters. New Donkey Breed Society rules mean that from 1st January 2004 only 4–8 year old stallions that 'are the offspring of a Stud Book stallion and a Stud Book mare OR will be a 3rd Generation Improving stallion' (Donkey Breed Society 2007) will be accepted.

All donkey owners are encouraged to get their animals registered with the DBS as they are then easier to sell and any progeny they have will be worth more and all new buyers and breeders are advised to select animals listed in the Stud Book or on one of the organisation's more general registers.

The Donkey Breed Society was originally established as the Donkey Show Society but it was slow to take off as its title inferred it was relevant only to owners wanting to show their animals. To broaden its appeal it changed its name to the Donkey Breed Society and has since gone from strength to strength. With an ever increasing membership, currently around 1,000, the DBS has been able to do much to raise the donkey's status not only by promoting good husbandry and management but by organising showing and driving classes, training days and special events and award schemes for its members. It also produces an array of publications covering all aspects of donkey care and a regular newsletter, Bray Talk, and anyone with access to the internet can find a huge range of donkey-related information on its new website at www.donkeybreedsociety.co.uk. The Society has become so influential that a separate section on it can be found later in the book, after the Donkey Driving section.

Although it generally encourages people to purchase donkeys, the Donkey Breed Society will usually strongly discourage them from breeding the animal as, although foals may be easy to sell, adult donkeys are not and thousands spend much of their lives in donkey refuges. Very few people in Britain now breed donkeys on a commercial scale and donkey owners are strongly advised to geld all males as a donkey stallion that is not allowed to breed can become very difficult and frustrated and, from a young age, can be extremely dangerous to have around. On sensing a mare in season, a stallion tends to bray loudly, regularly open and shut its mouth and become highly agitated. All its enclosures need to be remarkably robust as some have been known to jump or crash through a 5-barred gate. Given the chance, each stallion has the potential to sire up to 40 foals a year and its notoriously strong sex drive has lead to the phrases, 'hung like a donkey' and 'donkey rigged', to describe a well-endowed man.

If an owner does decide to breed from their donkey, brood mares should always be taken to a Stud Book registered stallion. A donkey stallion's reputation will be based on his pedigree, his success in the show ring and the quality of his progeny and a suitable match should be found by comparing the bloodlines and conformation faults of both parents. Advertisements for the top donkey studs in Britain can be found on the Donkey Breed Society's website. The Perehill Donkey Stud in Surrey is one donkey stud that claims all its stallions have 'superb temperaments and free flowing actions'. In contrast, the Trinitas Stud has a range of options from 12 year old Hercules of Trinitas who 'has a very broad chest, excellent limb conformation and bone to die for! (No cow hocks here)' to 4 year old Trinitas 'Enry 'Iggins who is described as 'a touch exuberant in the ring.' Currently in high demand are the services of 'Westra Patrick' who was judged Premium Stallion by the Donkey Breed Society in 2004. 'Westra Patrick' is advertised by his stud owners as 'a real mister versatile, rides, drives, eats, sleeps and dreams' and the '4x4 of the donkey world' with 'more than just a pretty face'. (Donkey Breed Society 2005)

No donkey, whether mare or stallion, should be allowed to breed until they are 3 or 4 years old and have grown to a good size. A donkey mare will come into season roughly every 3 weeks and will have a heat period of about 7 days during which she will let the stallion approach. Covering should take place in a small secure area or yard where there is no danger of escape and people must stand well clear of the action which can become very violent with the stallion biting the mare's neck causing her to kick out at him as he dismounts. To avoid any injury to the stallion it is best to pull him away sideways and as quickly as possible after the covering.

If a mare is tested in foal she should not be subject to stress and it may be better, where possible, to delay a long journey home for a few weeks. The typical gestation period for a donkey is 374 days but this can vary considerably and it is easy to be taken unawares if a mare foals early. When foaling is a few weeks away, a mare's udder starts swelling; when it is days away, her teats will become distended and when it is imminent she may become restless and stop eating. A foaling place, preferably a well-ventilated and drained stable with a bed of deep clean straw, must be prepared in good time.

Donkey mares are well able to foal on their own and it is best for people to stand quietly out of the way and only interfere if really necessary. The foal is born in a bag of amniotic fluid which should quickly burst so the baby donkey can take its first breath. It will also have a rubbery substance completely covering each of its tiny hooves but this will peel off within hours. The dam will pass the placenta and should then start to lick her foal. Licking stimulates both the foal and the flow of its mother's milk and it is essential that the first milk the foal receives is from its mother as this contains antibodies necessary for it to survive. Within moments of being born, the foal will begin to take its first steps although for about ten minutes its long, thin legs appear rubbery and shaky and it tends to collapse in all directions. After a good licking, its coat will be soft and woolly, its little mane, bristly, like a toothbrush, and its ridiculously large laid back ears should stand erect. Once the dam has recovered from the birth she loves to get into the paddock to have a roll.

For its first three months, a donkey foal is very vulnerable to the cold and wet and should be kept indoors at night. Its development is extremely rapid and it will soon be playfully running round its mother. It will have an inquisitive and mischievous nature and as it grows up shows an increasing interest in other animals and nibbles at anything it can reach. A foal will need its mother's milk for at least two months but within days of being born will also try grazing and eating a little hay. It will pester its mother for a drink even when she is asleep and after about four months it may well be time to wean it to give her a much needed break. Some mares will decide themselves when their foal has had enough milk and will then prevent it from suckling, in which case weaning occurs naturally, but foals whose mothers have plenty of milk will probably need to be forcibly weaned. In this instance one has to be cruel to be kind and a clean break is best even though it inevitably leads to mournful cries.

One behavioural trait that has been observed in donkeys, but not in horses, is that where there are a number of mares and foals together in a field, the mothers will elect a babysitter from amongst them. The chosen mare will be left to look after all the foals while the others go off to graze, perhaps for half an hour. (Borwick 1981)

For an ancient view of ass breeding we can turn to *The Husbandman's Instructor* of 1697. This states that,

> *the breeding of these creatures are in all particulars, the same with the mares, both in time and manner; and for a good breed, the male and female must be both of a reasonable age, large bodied, sound, and of a good kind. The male must be at least three years old; for from three to ten, they are very fit for breeding, though they bring forth their colts sometimes at two year, and a half; but it appears by the bad thriving, not to be so well, nor good for service or continuance.*
>
> *To make the she-ass retain the seed, you must, after she has been well leap'd, drive her up and down for an hour or more, a handsome pace. She seldom bringeth forth two at once, and appears to have a kind of shame in her delivery; for when she finds her burthen ready to come forth, she will, if possible, retire into some dark shady place, to avoid being seen. They bring forth their foal in a twelve month; and for a good breed it is convenient to let them be covered but once in two years, that they may bear kindly every other year. [...]*
>
> *The best covering time is from the twentieth of May to the tenth of June; and whilst they are with foal, they must not be greatly laboured, nor hard driven; but labour does the male good, for by reason of his extream lecherousness, he grows nought if he stands idle.'* (Speed 1697:112–117)

Memories of two Donkey Owners
Yolande Thompson-Royds (1912–2004)

Yolande Thompson-Royds was a devoted donkey owner who spent 40 years breeding and showing her animals and at the age of 92 was still winning medals with them. She was well known amongst the donkey owning fraternity in her beloved Yorkshire and was an active supporter of local donkey-related events. Her obituary appeared in the 2005 edition of *The Donkey*, the annual magazine of the Donkey Breed Society, and the following is a small part of her story.

One of Yolande's favourite donkeys, a mare called Bernadette, was born in 1971 to a jenny that had been brought over from Ireland in the 1950s. Bernadette was part of a religious dynasty; her father, who later became

Yolande Thompson-Royds with her beloved donkey, 1990.

Supreme Champion, was called Ascension and her elder siblings were Easter, Pentecost and Whitsun. Bernadette was named after the miracle-performing St Bernadette of Lourdes as, while she was still in the womb, her mother suffered from acute acorn poisoning and the vet said it would be a miracle if the foal was born alive. Now aged 30 plus, Yolande's favourite donkey regularly wins the Veterans' Rosette in county shows and is still, in her late owner's own words, 'as youthful as ever, full of fun and usually the ringleader at naughtiness'.

Bernadette has had six foals of her own, all of which became prize-winners, and in addition to her trips to the showground, has attended numerous local community events. One of these was the Palm Sunday Parade where she annually took the blessing for all the world's donkeys and another was the Disabled Children's Christmas party where she obligingly carried Father Christmas's sack. Over the years she and her owner entertained and befriended a huge range of people and raised over £1,000 for charity.

Derek Tangye (1912–1996)

In the 1960s, Derek Tangye wrote an enchanting novel, *The Donkey in the Meadow*, recalling the life he and his wife, Jeannie, led with their menagerie of animals on a Cornish daffodil farm. In addition to their two donkeys, Penny, a mare bred in the mountains of Connemara in Ireland, and her foal, Fred, born on the farm, Derek and Jeannie were joined by a cat called Llama, a muscovy drake, Boris, and three gulls, Knocker, Squeaker and Peter. Previous sections in this book (on donkey braying, body language, seeing and perceiving, and transport) have all referred to Tangye's novel so here are just two more passages, chosen as they concern several of his particularly poignant donkey memories.

The first describes Fred's:

> *first hee-haw and his first buttercup. He was a week old when he decided to copy his grazing mother, putting his nose to the grass without quite knowing what was expected of him. He roamed beside her sniffing importantly this*

grass and that; and then suddenly he saw the buttercup. A moment later he came scampering towards me with the buttercup sticking out of the corner of his mouth like a cigarette, and written all over his ridiculous face was: 'Look what I've found!'

The first hee-haw was to occur one afternoon in the autumn when Jeannie and I were weeding the garden. There was no apparent reason to prompt it. They were not far away from us in the meadow, and every now and then we had turned to watch them contentedly mooching around. And then came the sound.

It was at first like someone's maiden attempt to extract a note from a saxophone. It was a gasping moan. It then wavered a little, began to gain strength and confidence, started to rise in the scale, and then suddenly blossomed into a frenzied, hiccuping tenor-like crescendo.

'Heavens,' I said, 'What an excruciating noise!' (Tangye 1965: 81)

The second of Tangye's especially memorable donkey moments colourfully illustrates baby Fred's mischevious nature and occurred when two strangers walked innocently through the donkeys' field:

As I sat at my desk, I saw through the window a hatless elderly man come puffing up the path from the direction of the field, followed a moment later by a formidable looking lady. [...]

'Are those your damned donkeys in the field we've just come through?' barked the man. [...]

'Yes,' I replied doubtfully, 'anything wrong?'

'Very much so,' interrupted the lady grimly looking at me from under an old felt hat, 'the young one snatched my husband's cap and is running round the field with it.'

How had Fred managed it? Had he sneaked up behind the couple as they hurried along, annoyed they had taken no notice of him, and then performed a ballet dancer's leap to take the cap from the gentleman's head? [...]

I ran away from them laughing, down the path to the field, asking myself what I would have to do if Fred had gobbled it up. But as I did so I suddenly saw a galloping Fred coming towards me, tweed cap in mouth, and just behind him a thundering, rollicking Penny; and the two of them gave such an impression of joyous, hilarious elation that I only wished that Jeannie had been with me to see them.

The cap was intact, a little wet, but no sign of a tear; and when I thankfully returned it to its owner I asked what had happened. It was simple. It was almost as I imagined it. The couple had sat down on the grass to rest; and then up behind them came Fred. And away went the cap. (Tangye 1965: 114–115)

CHAPTER 7

Donkey-Related Leisure Activities

Riding

As a general rule, no donkey should carry over 50 kg (8 stone or 112 lb) or be ridden until it is four years old as before that age its skeleton has not properly formed and it may suffer 'dipped back' syndrome. Although a donkey mare or gelding makes an excellent mount for a small child, the animal's thin and bony back, low withers and shuffling gait makes it relatively uncomfortable to ride, especially if bareback, and its stubborn nature means it can be very disobedient. As it is hard to get a donkey to gallop or jump its popularity is usually limited to only the most novice of riders but some have been ridden over small jumps and even taken out hunting.

Before a donkey is ridden it should be properly tacked up with a well-fitting harness consisting of a bridle and saddle. A bridle is made up of leather bands running up the cheeks, over the head and around the brow, nose and throat, a rubber or metal bit that is held in the mouth and leather

Donkey riding, ca 1930.

Donkey riding, ca 1930.

Donkey-Related Leisure Activities | 117

Donkey as a suitable mount for children, ca 1975.

or rubber reins that connect this to the rider. The bit should be placed over the tongue and held in position by large rings at either side. If a donkey manages to get its tongue over the bit and the 'bit between its teeth', it can become too headstrong.

A simple donkey saddle may consist only of a felt pad placed on the withers and secured by a girth tightened under the belly. Iron stirrups should be hung by leather straps from metal bars positioned either side of the saddle and then adjusted to a length that enables a rider to sit upright in the saddle so that their ear, shoulder, hip and heel could all be joined by a straight vertical line. Saddle accoutrements can include a crupper that is fitted round the donkey's tail and attached to the back of the saddle to stop it sliding forward. As many animals violently object to having their tail threaded through this, it is advisable to stand close to the rump on the nearside when fitting it and try to slide it over the tail in one smooth motion.

Showing

The first recorded donkey shows in Britain were held for a few years in the 19th century in the Agricultural Hall in Islington, London. At that time the white 'Damascus Ass' with its large stature, easy paces and high speed was much admired and in 1866 the Prince of Wales won third prize at the Islington show with his giant white jack. Donkeys then fell out of fashion and were not really taken seriously again until after World War Two when some small clubs of donkey enthusiasts were set up. In the 1960s a well-known donkey aficionado, Robin Borwick, sparked off a new interest in the animal when he founded the Donkey Show Society, later renamed the Donkey Breed Society, to improve the donkey stock by encouraging better husbandry and management. The Society organised donkey shows around the country and, as standards rose and people began seeing the donkey looking its best, its status duly rose.

Today over 60 County Shows include donkey classes and every year there is a national competition to find the Supreme Champion Donkey. A show donkey is judged on its conformation, movement, presentation and manners and the following defects will all lose marks:

○ Too fat and heavy

○ Lopped ears

○ Small, light coloured or dull eyes

○ Roman nose

○ Small nostrils

○ Drooping lips

○ Weak neck that is 'dished' along its top edge

○ Too long a back or loins

○ Lopsided hind quarters

○ Weak or crooked legs with cow hocks (knees turned inward toward each other)

Donkey being put through its paces at the Great Yorkshire Show, 2003.

○ Pigeon toes (turned out in front or back)

The following are considered movement faults:

○ Plaiting (putting one foot in front of another)

○ Winging (extreme outward rotation of the limbs, also called paddling)

Donkey shows can include classes in leading, riding, driving and fancy dress and where there are a high number of entrants they may be divided into subclasses based on the breed or size of animal or age of handler. When the donkey's size is the determining factor, the typical class divisions are: miniatures (less than 9 hands high and not for riding); small standard (9–10.2 hands); large standard (10.2–12 hands) and large (over 12 hands). In America there may even be classes for mammoths (over 13½ hands). Classes for junior handlers are either lead-rein, riding or fancy dress and activity and are usually judged not so much on presentation as on obedience.

Show donkeys and their handlers need to be well groomed and behaved and any entire males must be kept well under control. In lead-rein classes, each competitor is required to bring their donkey into the ring, line it up for individual inspection and show off its paces. Judges may also ask for its feet to be lifted up. Donkeys should stand with their legs and feet well spaced, should not be reluctant to step forward, walk and trot and should change their gait smoothly with minimum encouragement from their handler. Use of a cane or schooling whip is allowed but this may result in a donkey moving in a crab like manner. All animals should wait patiently for their turn to step forward and should not be allowed to fall asleep.

Riding classes are usually held only for children. Competitors under 9 years old will have their donkey hand-led but those above that age must mount, walk and trot on their own. Any badly behaved mount that appears keen to make an early exit from the show ring can easily cause upset and embarrassment.

Driving classes may be only for carts of a traditional design, in which case turn-out is all important, or open to all vehicles, in which case non-traditional or exercise carts can be used and a donkey is judged mainly on its performance as a driving animal. Larger shows may include dressage trials and obstacle courses for drivers as well as 'Best Whip' tests in which the skill of the driver is the only thing that matters. In all driving classes the donkey, driver, cart and harness will be inspected for turnout and competitors must show they can walk, trot, steer and reverse on demand.

Success in the show ring will require that both the handler and their donkey are well attired. The current chairman of the Donkey Breed Society (DBS) Shows and Judges Committee suggests the following 'simple dress code:

○ *An excellent start would be white shirt worn with a Donkey Breed Society Tie, available from the DBS Shop*

○ *A plain or tweed jacket with a DBS badge or a discreet buttonhole or imitation cornflower worn in the buttonhole*

- *Beige trousers or an appropriate length plain or tweed skirt*

- *Flat heeled shoes in a subdued colour*

- *To complete this image a velour hat and gloves to match the shoes, and a smart leather covered or rattan cane no longer than 30 inches'* (Donkey Breed Society 2007)

One owner with much experience of showing donkeys considers that a hat is *'a must'* for ladies but *'not essential'* for a man. For everyone donning a hat, *'a brown bowler or a trilby looks good, or a flat cap with a matching jacket looks really well.'* (Tetlow 1997:319–334)

Dress for the donkey is determined in part by the restrictions of the handler's budget. Coloured nylon head collars are not considered appropriate for the show ring but rather a plain leather head collar or bridle. If a donkey is male its bridle may be embellished with brass and for the sake of safety it is essential that all entire males are shown in bridles with bits attached.

Driving

Donkeys can do more than just stand around in fields or go to shows and one of the main interests of many owners is driving. Donkey driving became popular in Victorian Britain when some were used to pull miniature carriages, wicker-work or basket 'phaetons' or sledges driven by children. A donkey could be trusted not to 'take off' as a pony might and even Queen Victoria in her later years drove a very smart donkey to a small carriage.

Today the Donkey Breed Society is a strong advocate of donkey driving and has established a special committee to put on training days and fun events around the country and actively encourage shows to hold driving classes for all levels of expertise. With rising numbers of entrants, donkey driving shows can be highly competitive and involve dressage trials or races over marathon and obstacle courses. Although most donkeys are driven singly, some classes are held for pairs (two donkeys driven side by side) and tandems (two donkeys driven one in front of the other).

Donkey harnessed to children's cart, ca 1930.

Donkey driving, ca 1980.

Donkey-Related Leisure Activities | 123

Occasionally there is the opportunity to see a Unicorn (three donkeys driven together, one in front as a leader and two behind side by side) and a team where four donkeys are driven together.

In comparison to show classes, non-competitive donkey driving events such as rallies are informal and relaxed affairs, a chance for a friendly chat and glass of sherry. Rally courses are usually 6–8 miles long and are planned by enthusiasts who often opt for a drive starting from their own homes. Calm donkeys make good driving animals for people of all ages and abilities and in Britain the Riding for the Disabled Association has set up increasingly popular disabled driving groups.

On a level road, the average donkey can pull at a trot a vehicle weighing up to 128kg (20 stone) plus a medium sized adult or two children. A donkey driving cart should be as light as possible with the shafts long enough to prevent the cart from bumping against the donkey's legs when travelling downhill and set well enough apart to prevent it rubbing against the donkey's sides. Although at the top end of the market there are some particularly elegant private driving vehicles and immaculate leather harnesses, many donkey drivers make do with a basic exercise cart and sturdy webbing harness. The standard components of a driving harness are a bridle, a back pad or saddle secured by a girth, a breast collar that buckles around the neck and a breeching that wraps around the hindquarters. The saddle, breast collar and breeching all support the cart and attach it to the donkey while the reins of the bridle connect donkey with driver. Straps, known as traces, that attach the breast collar to the two poles or shafts of the cart enable forward motion while straps joined to the breast collar and breeching transmit a reverse draught and are used for braking and reversing. For the cart to be properly balanced, the shafts need to be held level by 'tugs' that are attached to each side of the saddle. If a donkey, once constrained by all its straps, bands and collars, etc., still proves skittish, then bridle winkers or blinkers can be added to shield its eyes.

When it comes to the driver's outfit, the full kit for showing consists of a hard hat, gloves, sturdy shoes, blanket over the knees and whip. Although properly called 'the whip', the driver should use only a light switch to reprimand the donkey by touching it between the pad and the collar. Some drivers assert control using verbal commands such as 'walk on', 'halt', 'walk on again' and 'trot' whilst others try whistling. Words of encouragement will boost a donkey's morale and should always be used during training.

As one might imagine, controlling a headstrong and stubborn donkey from the seat of a cart requires patience and skill and this is reflected in the belief that to dream of driving a donkey signifies that all your energies and pluck will be brought into play against a desperate effort on the part of enemies to overthrow you. If you are in love, it is said that evil women will cause you trouble. (Parker 2007)

Racing

Donkey races, otherwise known as donkey derbies, are often highly entertaining with riders usually having little control over the speed and direction of their mounts. The donkey's stubborn nature means the odds

Student donkey race at the Royal Agricultural College, ca 1887, with costumes of a black & white minstrel, transvestite and fool – all characters associated with the carnivalesque underworld of the donkey.

are pretty unpredictable although some race goers maintain that males usually win. Donkey derbies are always popular community events that attract large crowds and can be lucrative fund raising opportunities. The annual donkey derby held each spring at Burnham Park in Buckinghamshire is one of the best attended in the country and all the money it raises goes to Cancer Care charities.

In the 19th Century a donkey derby was part of the annual sports day at the Royal Agricultural College in Cirencester. Students in fancy dress raced donkeys over about half a mile and a race card was printed setting out the terms and conditions and listing the names of all entrants. In 1905, competitors for the 'Grand '"Ass You Don't Like It"' or 'Great Unseatem Stakes' included 'Gone away' ridden by 'Farm labourer', 'President Kruger' ridden by 'A Shepherd' and 'Two lovely black eyes' with 'Chinaman' on board. One of the race rules stated that 'only donkeys that have been regularly flogged by Members of the R.A.C at least five minutes previous to the race are eligible'. We can infer from this that little attention was paid to the plight of the donkeys and the event has long since been discontinued.

Donkey racing is also popular abroad and in Trinidad an annual donkey derby held by the Rotary Club in the town of Arima involves six heats and a grand final. The riders, who wear numbered vests, are usually professional jockeys from the Arima Race Club while the donkeys are all named and equipped with blinkers to increase their chances. Consistent good form has been shown by 'Hurricane' who has recently taken the triple, winning the race every year from 2000–2003.

Trinidadian race-goers maintain that 'contrary to the myths, stubbornness is not the only personality trait a donkey can possess' and Hurricane's owner has found that one of his other donkeys, 'Smallie', has a such a calming influence that she is always taken along to act as a companion to Hurricane. Were she not there Hurricane would become restless and irritated and be 'impossible to control'. (Sankar-Oyan 2005)

CHAPTER 8

Protection of Donkeys

Cruelty to Donkeys

Due to over-hunting and competition for food and water with humans and their livestock, the donkey's wild ancestor, the African wild ass, is now all but extinct in the wild. In contrast, the domestic donkey is very much alive and well. Within its overall flourishing population, however, there are those that are subjected to harsh treatment by societies where their status is very low. Unfortunately many donkeys in the Developing World are poorly cared for, often because their owners are barely able to feed and house themselves, let alone their animals. Those that suffer most stress tend to live in and around towns where there is a lot of competition for food and people have little experience of working with animals. In arid, remote and mountainous areas where people are more dependent on their donkeys they tend to look after them better; for example, the Samburu, a pastoral community in northern Kenya, recognise that the branches of certain trees are too hard to use as whips.

One case that serves to illustrate the sort of ill treatment some working donkeys have to endure is described below by Dr Valliyate Manilal who works as a vet in India: *'There are thousands of brick kilns around Delhi. Each donkey may carry its own bodyweight in bricks in temperatures as high as 50C for up to 12 hours a day. Each donkey travels about 14km a day, hauling bricks from the area where they are made to the furnace. The land is not flat and this makes walking with loads very difficult. By the end of the brick-making season, animals are often lame and exhausted. Many are abandoned and die. The life of these donkeys may be no more than two years.'* (Manilal, Valliyate 2004)

Cruelty to donkeys is not just restricted to the Developing World and the following countries all have a record of maltreatment: Spain, Greece, Turkey, Egypt, Iraq, Iran, Australia, Galapagos Islands, Jamaica and Mexico. In most of these, the abuse is not a result of poverty but more a desire to ridicule. In Iran, in 2003, a court punished vandals by ordering them to ride around their neighbourhood on donkeys, facing backwards. This, apparently, drew a crowd of curious, if slightly baffled, onlookers. In Spain, a small village situated in the Caceres region traumatises donkeys on a worrying scale as part of a traditional event, known as the 'Fiesta of Villanueva de la Vera', held every Shrove Tuesday. During the fiesta, meant to celebrate the one-time capturing of a rapist, a donkey that has been force-fed alcohol is mounted by the largest, fattest man of the village and then mocked by a drunken mob while being dragged by a long rope through the cobbled streets. Tradition maintains that the animal be tormented and beaten until it collapses and is then crushed to death by the crowd. As a result of protests from animal welfare groups both inside and outside the country, the villagers have now agreed not to kill the donkey but they still subject it to the terrifying ordeal of being mobbed in the streets.

The Donkey Sanctuary

By far the most important protector of donkeys in Britain and many other countries is the Donkey Sanctuary. Based near Sidmouth in Devon, England, this is the largest donkey refuge in the world that, over the course of 30 years, has grown from a single caring owner with one lonely donkey to a worldwide organisation of over 300 staff that owns some 1,100 acres of land and has rescued more than 11,000 donkeys in the UK and Ireland.

The Donkey Sanctuary was founded in 1969 by Dr Elisabeth Svendsen after she acquired a homeless donkey to act as companion to one she had already. She then found room for several other destitute donkeys and soon discovered there were many more out there that, for one reason or another, had lost their homes or owners. As news of unwanted donkeys accumulated, Dr Svendsen determined to do something to help them; she began fundraising in order to buy more land and the Donkey Sanctuary was born. As well as encountering many animals in need of a refuge, Dr Svendsen also found an incredible passion for donkeys amongst the general public and this, luckily, translated into donations and more hands-on volunteers. In 1973, when over 200 destitute animals were bequeathed to her, Dr Svendsen made the Donkey Sanctuary a registered Charity with the aim of preventing the suffering of donkeys through the provision of high quality, professional advice, training and support on donkey welfare.

Today the Donkey Sanctuary is fortunate enough to be able to guarantee permanent sanctuary to any donkey in the UK and Ireland that needs it and is proud to claim that 'no donkey is ever refused admittance'. It currently looks after more than 3,000 donkeys in Britain of which 500 are kept at its main farm and headquarters in Sidmouth, Devon. The Sanctuary owns 10 other farms and over a third of its staff have worked there for over 10 years. About 1,500 of the donkeys under the care of the Sanctuary in the UK are not housed on its farms but are fostered out to approved and registered carers on a semi-permanent basis. The large fostering scheme run by the Donkey Sanctuary enables many of its younger and fitter animals to find a good home – the donkeys remain under the ownership of the Sanctuary and are regularly visited in their foster homes by Welfare Officers.

An average of 6 new donkeys a week are taken in by the Donkey Sanctuary. There is a strict policy of no breeding on any of its farms and stallions are castrated soon after arriving. Any pregnant mares that are brought in are foaled at the Sanctuary and their foal offered the same lifetime protection guarantee as its mother. All new arrivals to the Sanctuary's headquarters in Sidmouth spend 6 to 8 weeks in the Isolation Unit where they receive full veterinary checks, inoculations and farrier treatment and are assessed to see which group of donkeys and which farm would suit them best – some may be found to have a favourite food that can be used as a treat while others may have certain behavioural problems that need to be addressed. In one case a donkey arriving at the Sanctuary was found to be addicted to alcohol, a result of being given a pint every night to entertain a pub landlord's customers, and had to be given beer to begin with, before it could be weaned off.

As donkeys often form strong bonds with one another, no animal is ever separated from a companion arriving from the same home, though in time some may form new friendships with others that are closer in age. While at the Sanctuary, all donkeys are fitted with a collar that is colour coded to indicate their sex and any special needs and labelled with their name and intake number. Each one is also given a microchip for identification and security purposes.

As well as caring for donkeys in the, Dr Elisabeth Svendsen is concerned about those abroad, many of which suffer appalling neglect and abuse. The majority of these are in Developing Countries where donkeys are often overworked and their owners are too poor to care for them. In response to this, Dr Svendsen established the International Donkey Protection Trust (IDPT) which worked to provide free veterinary treatment and education for donkey owners. To simplify administration, the IDPT was incorporated into the Donkey Sanctuary in 2000 and the aims and objects of the new, amalgamated Charity are 'the provision of care, protection and/or permanent security anywhere in the world for donkeys and mules which are in need of attention by reason of sickness, maltreatment, poor circumstances, ill-usage or other like causes, and the prevention of cruelty and suffering among donkeys and mules.' The Donkey Sanctuary currently runs overseas projects in Ethiopia, Mexico, Kenya, India, Egypt, and Spain and provides an average of 97,000 free veterinary treatments every year. It strives to investigate reports of cruelty to donkeys anywhere in the world either through its own overseas staff or any other of its many contacts.

In 1989 Dr Svendsen founded a third donkey-related charity known as the Elisabeth Svendsen Trust for Children and Donkeys (EST) to enable children with special needs to benefit both physically and emotionally from meeting and riding the donkeys. The success of the EST has been highly acclaimed and it certainly provides a way in which donkeys at the Sanctuary can return the favours given them by society. The first specially designed riding centre was constructed by the Trust at the Sidmouth Donkey Sanctuary and there are now three others around the country, in Birmingham, Leeds and Manchester, each of which is attended by up to 150 children a week.

The work of the EST has proved conclusively that grooming, stroking and riding a donkey has a direct calming and confidence-boosting influence on even the most disturbed or withdrawn child. It also helps to

Donkey therapy session at the Elizabeth Svendsen Trust for Children and Donkeys, Sidmouth, Devon, 2004.

improve balance and strengthen weak muscles and even children with severe cerebral palsy have significantly increased their mobility. The Trust's riding classes include exercises and games tailored to suit each child's needs and are run by qualified instructors with many willing volunteers on hand to offer support. Those attending the therapy sessions range from one year-olds to young adults and anyone too heavy to ride the donkeys can be taught to drive a small cart.

For those who would like to experience the Donkey Sanctuary at first hand, its main farm in Sidmouth is open to the public 365 days a year from 9 a.m. till dusk. There is no entrance charge and anyone is welcome to walk round the premises, talk to the donkeys and spend time in the information centre, shop and restaurant. While the majority of donkeys are out grazing in the fields during the summer months, the geriatrics remain in the main yard and the stables house donkeys with special diets and needs. A small group of blind donkeys have a padded paddock to stop

Geriatric donkey barn at the Donkey Sanctuary, Sidmouth, Devon, 2004.

them injuring themselves and the oldest resident, aged 57, is provided with extra heating and special shoes to guard against a fatal foot condition.

A trip to the Donkey Sanctuary is a chance to witness animal care at its very best. Donkeys who need medical treatment are given sweetened sandwiches in which the medication is hidden to make it more palatable. There is a specially equipped donkey hospital on site where sick animals are tended to by eight full-time vets and five veterinary nurses. The Donkey Sanctuary runs free training courses in basic donkey health care and management and anyone can learn more about the organisation or donkeys in general at the Information Centre which is well stocked with displays, leaflets and videos. The shop contains an incredible range of donkey goods from a donkey chess set and desk tidy to a 'Super Donk Kite'.

The Donkey Sanctuary is visited by about 160,000 people each year and has over 200,000 on its mailing list who each receive two newsletters a year and mail order catalogues. Unusually for a charity, and especially for one so large and active, there is no membership fee, no government aid and no charge for admission or parking – it is entirely funded by voluntary donations and legacies and receives over £14 million a year.

As fundraisers, donkeys appear to have the winning formula – we seem more willing to ease their plight than we do that of our fellow humans. Such generosity may be explained partly by the fact that Britons traditionally see it as the duty of the state to look after sick people and partly by the amount of people that the Donkey Sanctuary involves in its work. A team of the most friendly donkeys is regularly taken round hospices and retirement homes where elderly residents have a chance to get to know them – one of the smallest has even been taken upstairs to visit a lady at her bedside. The Charity's founder, Dr Elisabeth Svendsen, explains her donors' generosity by the fact that they know nearly all their money goes direct to the donkeys – the organisation's administration costs are very low, just 6p in £1. This is certainly one reason for the Donkey Sanctuary's residents attracting such a remarkable amount of money but it is surely just part of the answer and a fuller explanation of our depth of feeling for the donkey will be sought in a later section of the book that looks at how it is portrayed to us from an early age in literature, lore and legend.

Society for the Protection of Animals Abroad (SPANA)

SPANA works in some of the poorest countries in the world and treats some of the working donkeys in greatest suffering. Its aims are to provide free veterinary care to working animals and educate children and owners on how to care for them properly thus making cruelty to animals a thing of the past. With 19 veterinary centres and 21 mobile clinics, SPANA treated over 300,000 animals in 2007 throughout North and West Africa and the Middle East. (SPANA 2008)

The charity was set up in the 1920s by Kate Hosali and her daughter Nina, after they saw the mistreatment of animals on their travels through North Africa. They couldn't bear the thought of working animals suffering needlessly and so Kate returned, as soon as possible, to treat as many as she could, while Nina set up SPANA in London.

In a time when a woman travelling alone was disapproved of, Kate worked tirelessly on her own in foreign lands. Initially, she was ridiculed but she persevered and won the respect and friendship of the local people. An extract from a letter of Kate Hosali dated 1925 tells how she began by treating a single donkey in the market place and became inundated for days with thousands of donkeys needing her help. This is on the SPANA website (www.spana.org) as is a video of Kate's first visit to North Africa.

The Donkey Breed Society (DBS)

The Donkey Breed Society (DBS) has already been mentioned under the subheadings of Donkey Breeding, Showing and Driving but, as a 'charity working for all donkeys', its work is broader than this and it merits a separate chapter to itself. The aim of the DBS is to enable everyone to get maximum enjoyment from their donkey while ensuring the donkeys themselves are properly cared for. To this end, it offers a huge range of advice and products and organises events such as shows for donkey owners to meet and share information.

DBS Donkey Proficiency Tests

To encourage good donkey management the Society runs its own proficiency tests ranging from 'Introductory (minimum age 6 years)' with the objective of getting 'to know your donkey' to 'Gold (minimum age 16 years)' for which 'a thorough knowledge of the donkey' must be displayed. The 'Advanced Riding Test (juniors only according to weight/height limitations)' demands 'a balanced seat independent of reins' and an understanding of 'elementary aids' while the dressage qualification requires proof of an 'obedient and willing' mount.

DBS Active Donkey Award Scheme

The DBS's 'Active Donkey Award Scheme', open to members of all ages, recognises that 'most donkeys, be they young or old, big or small, will benefit both physically and mentally from a change of scene and a break from the usual routine' (Donkey Breed Society 2007). To qualify for an Award Scheme certificate and special rosette, a donkey has to complete eight different activities over a one year period. Taking part in a breed showing class will not count as an activity but the Donkey Breed Society gives the following examples which all will:

○ Helping out at various charity events

○ Visiting schools and old people's homes

○ Taking part in Palm Sunday processions, Nativity plays and various parades

○ Going for pleasure walks and drives

○ Carrying their owners' shopping and helping to deliver parish magazines

○ Appearing at Fairs, Fetes, children's parties and coffee mornings

○ Assisting in demonstrations to show correct grooming and showing techniques and general donkey management

○ Hauling logs and helping to carry in the vegetable harvest

To encourage continued interest by its members, the DBS pledges that 'when a donkey has achieved three (not necessarily consecutive) years in the scheme they receive a special engraved plaque and there are now plans – to be announced – for further awards.' (Donkey Breed Society 2007)

DBS 'Donkey Weekend'

For all donkey devotees in Britain, the Donkey Breed Society holds a 'Donkey Weekend' every summer which it markets as 'The Complete Donkey Experience'. Along with a multitude of donkeys and their owners, many spectators turn out to enjoy separate show classes for donkey geldings, colts, fillies, mares, stallions, foals, young handlers and the British Supreme Driving Champion. Images of the winners and runners up in all classes can be seen on the DBS website at www.donkeybreedsociety.co.uk.

Over the course of the Donkey Weekend there are also donkey rides, talks, demonstrations, junior quizzes and colouring competitions and 'plenty of shopping opportunities'. (Donkey Breed Society 2007) Donkey themed items and official DBS products can always be purchased remotely on the DBS online shop whose stock includes, 'a selection of donkeys from fluffy to silver', 'useful donkey themed household gadgets', 'lovely jewellery from cufflinks to brooches' and 'miscellaneous [objects] from clocks to cushions'.

DBS Junior Section

To ensure continued support for the organisation, the DBS gets children involved by having a special Juniors Committee to represent the under 16s on the DBS Council. By taking part in the DBS Active Donkey Award Scheme, described above, children can accumulate points towards badges, certificates and a place in the DBS Roll of Honour. They can also attend residential camps with their donkeys to make friends with other young donkey fans and 'learn the ropes' from their elders. A dedicated Juniors' Section with well illustrated reports of children's activities as well as some amusing stories, poems and jokes, sometimes written by junior members themselves, is included in the DBS newsletter, Bray Talk, while those with access to a computer can 'play the ee-awesome donkey tail game'.

CHAPTER 9

Donkeys in Literature, Legend and Lore

Introduction

Just pause for a minute and picture a donkey in your mind's eye. What you see will depend very much on where in the world you live. Most in the affluent West probably envisage a passive animal grazing contentedly in a field or standing rather forlornly on a beach. Those who are owners may recall a more spirited creature that looks up with ears pricked as someone approaches or obstinately digs in its heels and lays back its ears on being led towards the stable. In Developing Countries and medieval Europe where the working donkey is or was part of everyday life most people will imagine a heavily laden beast and anyone who has encountered a sexually-aroused donkey stallion will certainly reflect on its aggressive and violent streak. Attitudes in Victorian Britain varied according to people's status and in 1916 Wilson called the donkey 'the plaything of a richer man's children or the slave of some costermonger'. (cited by Hall & Clutton-Brock 1995)

Different cultures indicate their varying attitudes towards the donkey by portraying it differently in traditional folklore and giving its name alternative meanings. Languages that contain a large number of donkey terms are likely to develop where the donkey features prominently in everyday life and when many of these are defamatory the animal is most likely to be seen as ridiculous and stupid. Out of 53 of the most commonly spoken languages today, the following have significantly more alternative meanings for donkey than any other: Albanian, Romanian, Turkish, Ukranian and Japanese. Three of these are Eastern European and here the donkey does, indeed, still play a significant part of everyday life. The Romanians have four modern words which in English are translated simply as 'donkey' and over a hundred listed alternative meanings of the word ranging from 'addle-brained' to 'zombie'. In Arab countries such as Iraq it has always been impolite to utter the word for 'ass' unless it is at once neutralised by some deprecatory phrase meaning

© PHOTOGRAPH BY M SPROT

The donkey as 'The plaything of a richer man's children' (Wilson, 1916), ca 1900 'if you will excuse me mentioning such a thing?' They must think of it as not only stupid but also dirty and of very low status. The Japanese, on the other hand, appear to view the donkey more as a loudmouth than an ignoramus – 'donkey' in their language is also used to refer to 'a patient's call button in a hospital' and 'the firing of guns'. (Parker 2007)

Most English terms and phrases containing the word 'donkey' allude to a working animal that does jobs of secondary importance. Examples are:

○ Donkey engine: a small auxiliary engine used for subsidiary work

○ Donkey jacket: a thick jacket worn by manual labourers as protection against the weather

○ Donkey work: ground work or drudgery

○ Nodding donkey: machine relentlessly performing repetitive and thankless tasks

Other names and adages stem from what we see as the donkey's most distinctive physical and behavioural traits. These include:

○ Donkey orchid: an orchid with two upper petals sticking straight up like a donkey's ears

○ Jackass hare: any one of several species of American hares with very long ears

○ Jackass penguin: an African penguin with a call resembling a donkey's bray

○ 'Talk the hind legs off a donkey': to talk incessantly – a donkey's hind legs are its source of strength, so to talk thus is to tire out one's listener

○ 'Haud the cuddy [Scottish for ass] reeking': make constant exertion – used in relation to any business

Connotations of the word 'ass' are similar in Britain and America and the word is used interchangeably with 'arse' to insult ('you stupid ass')

or demean ('what a smart ass').

A further indication of our viewing the donkey as the poor relation to the horse is the vocabulary used to refer to its different life stages. Male and female donkeys are known as jacks and jennies respectively but there are no terms referring specifically to a young donkey or to a castrated male. The horse has been assigned a relatively rich descriptive vocabulary including mare, stallion, gelding, filly and foal but the donkey must borrow most of these and then add the word 'donkey' to distinguish itself from the seemingly superior species.

It is probably fair to say that throughout history people from all cultures have seen the donkey as an animal that carries the burdens of others and as such have thought it either pitiable or contemptible, depending on the circumstances.

An Object of Pity

O God,
Let me appear before You with these beasts
Whom I so love because they bow their heads
Sweetly, and halting join their little feet
So gently that it makes you pity them.
    (Francis Jammes)

And when that donkey looked me in the face,
His face was sad! And you are sad, my Public!
    (Smith, James & Horace Ib. 'Playhouse Musings')

The donkey has always inspired a degree of pity, as though there is something miserable and morose about the animal. Indeed, in its early days, the donkey's lot was not a happy one. Often half-starved and neglected, left to forage for itself on odd patches of grass and weeds, its feet growing long and splitting for lack of attention, tolerating gross maltreatment, cruelty, over-work, and no respect or affection from its handler, it is not surprising the donkey seemed so down at heel.

The archetypal 'poor old grey donkey' is AA Milne's Eeyore who seems permanently depressed and lives on the fringes of 100 Aker Wood in a 'gloomy place rather boggy and sad'. Eeyore is the main character in two of the 'Winnie the Pooh' stories: one in which he loses his tail and one in which he has a birthday which everyone has forgotten. In the first of these Pooh Bear comes across Eeyore standing by himself gazing sadly at the ground and informs him that his tail is missing – Eeyore hasn't noticed and sighs heavily. When Pooh then offers to find it for him Eeyore is mildly surprised as he thought he didn't have any 'real friends'. Pooh's search takes him to Owl's house where he notices a new bell-rope that appears rather familiar. Owl had found it hanging over a bush and assumed nobody wanted it but Pooh then recognises it as Eeyore's tail. Christopher Robin nails it back to its rightful place whereupon Eeyore surprises everyone by frisking happily around the forest. The story of Eeyore's lost tail has inspired a traditional children's party game in which blindfolded contestants take turns to try attach a tail to the right place on a cut-out donkey.

The tale of Eeyore's birthday begins with him staring forlornly at his reflection in a stream and pondering on how pathetic it is that nobody cares enough to have remembered it was his birthday – 'the happiest day of the year' he cynically informs Pooh. Pooh then feels so sorry for him that he rushes off to 'get poor Eeyore a present of *some* sort at once, and he could always think of a proper one afterwards'. The story culminates in Eeyore receiving just two presents: a burst balloon from Piglet and an empty honey pot from Pooh and then amusing himself by 'taking the balloon out, and putting it back again, as happy as could be …' (Milne 1926)

The donkey's gloomy nature was acknowledged in an early veterinary book, *The Husbandman's Instructor*, written in 1697 which stated, '*by reason of the melancholy quality that abounds in them [asses], they among all creatures, if any thing at all, are the least delighted in musick; and for the same reason troubled with fearful dreams, which make them not only groan and make piteous noise in their sleep, but also, if they lie near any hard thing, to beat their feet and heads, whereby they much hurt and bruise themselves; but much more those of their kind, that lie near them.*' (Speed

1697:112–117) This book even prescribed a cure for melancholia and this can be found in the section on medication.

Part of the reason we automatically feel pity for the donkey is due to its association with oppression and abject poverty. Television and newspaper coverage of famine and destitution around the world nearly always includes harrowing pictures of donkeys caught up in the human suffering and we are often left concerned about the animals, as well as about the people. So cynical are many people about political organisations that they may feel that giving money to charities that care for the donkeys will better relieve suffering than a donation to a human agency such as the Communist party or Resistance movements.

Even though in Britain donkeys rarely feature in our daily lives, such self-effacing and doleful animals sometimes receive sympathy out of proportion to their needs. Animal charities caring for donkeys receive healthy donations and their adverts are heavily loaded with depictions of lonely and harshly treated animals. Donkeys induce sympathy partly because they look like second-rate horses and partly by appearing so gloomy and tired of life. A visitor to the Donkey Sanctuary, a Charity which cares for thousands of abandoned animals and receives huge voluntary donations sums up what many of us feel, '[donkeys] are like teddy bears, all furry with big eyes and they always look so sad'.

Woolly, gentle, friendly animals will, of course, attract our concern and this is just how donkeys are portrayed in most children's storybooks which form part of our earliest memories. The 'poor little donkey' is introduced to us long before we become worldly wise and cynical and even those who rarely encounter the real thing are likely to feel pity for it throughout their life. Children are thought to love donkeys partly because they are about the right size for them to make eye contact with whilst women are thought to have a closer affiliation with them than men as donkeys can behave quite like small children being playful, attention seeking and mischievous.

A series of children's books that illustrate the loving, soft and cuddly depiction of the donkey are Peter Clover's *Donkey Diaries* (2001) which tell of children rescuing abandoned donkeys and giving them a new life at a sanctuary. Two books from the series are *Donkey Drama* in which a little blind donkey is rescued from an old scrap yard and *Donkey in Distress* in which a donkey foal is saved from the brink of disaster. Each concludes with the donkeys living happily in the sanctuary where the oldest resident *'was very gentle and quiet and liked to sleep a lot with one eye slightly open, keeping the rest of the group in close sight'.* (Clover 2002)

'Donkey's Glory' by Nan Goodall (1944) is a children's book that relates the Biblical tale of the donkey. This features a little grey donkey who after wearily carrying Mary to Bethlehem is bullied in the stable by the camels brought by the visiting three kings. It then makes the 'Donkey Promise of Obedience' to Joseph and helps him and his family to flee from the evil King Herod. The donkey bears a little foal that grows up to witness Jesus bringing a little girl back to life. This in turn gives birth to a 'snow-white' foal which as an adult has the honour of carrying Jesus into Jerusalem. When this little white donkey hears that his master has been attacked and killed he is so upset that 'great, heavy tears rolled down his face, making deep furrows in his furry cheeks'. The story ends with the 'risen again' Jesus appearing to thank him for his loyalty and declare he 'shall be known from now onwards, for ever and ever, as Laban the Kingbearer.'. (Goodall 1944)

The fact that children and their parents love donkeys is not lost on advertisers and celebrities seem to love the long-eared pet. In recent years a 'Win a Donkey Ribena orignal' competition has been launched with purchasers receiving either a blow-up donkey or a real life animal which will be looked after at the Donkey Sanctuary. In Mexico youngsters also learn to associate donkeys with treats as a result of a traditional game in which a toy donkey is found stuffed with sweets.

A Lowly Being

It is probably fair to say that wherever the horse and donkey exist together, the donkey is often seen as being second-rate – a sort of asinine dustbin. In England its humble status seems to have been established from the moment of its introduction by the Romans; they viewed it as their servant and this attitude was accepted without question by the native people. To dream of someone riding a donkey is said to denote a meagre inheritance and the following two 17th-century English proverbs signify a lowly status: 'An ass is but an ass, though laden with gold' and 'If an ass goes a-travelling, he'll not come home a horse'.

The Golden Ass written by Apuleius towards the end of the second century AD, is a tale of allegory, satire and bawdiness as seen through the eyes of a young man who was transformed into a donkey and passed from owner to owner encountering a desperate gang of robbers and being forced to perform lewd 'human' tricks. When subjected to rough treatment, the man as donkey determined that, 'the weight of my load, huge as it was, did not trouble me: I was to glad to get away from that awful fellow'. Verbal abuse, however, provoked a different reaction and on hearing itself insulted once too often the donkey, 'wondered if I shouldn't start bucking as if possessed'. (Kennedy 1998)

Many nationalities view the donkey as being a typical sidekick, a close friend or crony who assists a partner in a superior position. Two examples are the Hollywood invention 'Shrek', a digital ogre with a donkey companion, described later, and the Spaniard's 'Sancho Panza', a deceptively fore-sighted donkey-rider who tried to save his master, Don Quixote, from hare-brained schemes, such as confronting windmills.

Aesop's fables, which date from the early 6th century BC use the imaginary adventures of animals to make a moral point about human life, as relevant today as ever. The following is one of these tales that portrays the donkey as something that should know better than to have ideas above its station:

Asinine Pride

An ass was being driven into town with a statue of a god mounted on his back. When the passers-by did obeisance to the statue, the ass imagined that it was he to whom they showed this respect, and he was so elated that he started to bray and refused to budge a step further. His driver, taking in the situation, laid on with his stick. 'Wretch!' he cried, 'that would be the last straw, for men to bow down to an ass.'

When people boast of honours that do not rightfully belong to them, they make themselves a laughing-stock to those who know them.

The Sacred Donkey

In the Bible the donkey is a dependably solid presence in hard times. The most common Greek word for ass, Hamor, appears roughly 100 times in the early Greek translation of the Biblical text and the ownership of many donkeys is a sign of God's blessing. In seeming contrast, however, God chose to speak through a donkey to show Balaam the folly of his ways. The Bible often specifies whether someone is riding a donkey since this would indicate their status. Joseph, being a poor man, used a donkey to carry his wife and child and Jesus rode a donkey into Jerusalem as it was appropriate transport for a humble man. The following verse predicting the events leading up to Jesus' death exemplifies the donkey's Biblical role *'Behold, thy King cometh unto thee; he is just and having salvation; lowly and riding on an ass, and upon a colt the foal of an ass.'* (Zechariah 9 v.9) (Eadie ed.1960)

The belief that a donkey carried Christ into Jerusalem on Palm Sunday has given rise to the popular myth of how the donkey got the cross mark on its back. The tale goes that after carrying its master into the city, the donkey came to the hill of Calvary where it witnessed the tragic crucifixion. The donkey wished that it had been able to carry the cross for Jesus as it was the proper one to carry heavy burdens. As a reward for its loyalty the Lord caused the shadow of the cross to fall across the donkey's back and left it there for it to carry forevermore.

Pet donkey carrying Mary in Church role, 2007.

The Christian belief that the donkey was present at the birth of Jesus has led to it being included in most nativity scenes and pictured on many Christmas cards and its link with Palm Sunday and Easter Day means it sometimes attends outreach events on these Christian holy days. In the 'Thanksgiving for the Animals Service' held in 2004 at the Cathedral Church in Gloucester the donkey played a central role. During the service a donkey stood patiently at the altar and afterwards people were invited to take their own animals into the church to receive a blessing. The proceedings included the following 'Prayer of the Donkey': *Dear God, I am your servant the Donkey. Thank you for making me tough and strong. Thank you for those who laugh with me and look after me. Lord – you gave me a will of my own: but help me to listen to your whisperings and to do what you want. Amen.* Hymns, prayers and readings were accompanied by pageants celebrating the part played by the donkey in the life of Jesus and donkey rides were then given with each rider receiving a brochure entitled 'I rode a donkey like someone special rode a donkey'.

The ceremony was meant to revive an ancient tradition known as the 'Feast of Asses' or 'Feast of Fools' which was popular in France and England during the Middle Ages. Although usually held in a cathedral, however, this was far from being a reverent occasion – more a kind of clerical Saturnalia. It began with a carnival-like procession through the streets headed by a richly caparisoned donkey carrying a young woman and child. On its arrival at the Cathedral the donkey was made to stand beside the high altar as part of a bawdy and drunken Mass in which braying often took the place of the customary responses. The event was accompanied by obscene jests and dances and the fact that the donkey was a central feature signified its link with the Greek wine-god, Bacchus, and drunken behaviour. The Feast of the Asses took place in the middle of January and was possibly an antidote for gloom as people outside the Mediterranean regions tended to associate the donkey with the sunny South.

The donkey's religious association makes it ideal for more spiritual work and the Donkey Ministry in Tasmania and Australia uses what it calls the 'charismatic, magnetic presence of the gentle donkey' as an evangelical means of attracting church-goers by parading it through the streets before a church service. As with anything involving donkeys, however, such events do not always go according to plan and one that did not is recounted by the author Justin Cartwright in his book *The Promise of Happiness* (2004). In this a donkey, a 'bony, dusty, biblical creature', when asked to trot 'took umbrage' and set off at a 'fast and determined scuttle' before ducking under a barrier to escape. Its leader concluded that 'donkeys are intractable and highly unsuitable for children' and when Jesus rode a donkey 'maybe [he] didn't try to make it trot!' (Cartwright 2004)

As well as being linked to Jesus Christ, the ass was associated with the Egyptian god, Ra, and the Greek god Dionysus. Dionysus (Bacchus) is the mythological Greek wine-god who in ancient art is often pictured lilting tipsily on the back of an ass. In Greece the donkey has always been linked to viticulture as it has worked in vineyards since the 1st millenium BC. Appropriately, Dionysus is not only the patron of boozers but also of hard-working vine-growers and wine-makers. Once they got to know it better, the Ancient Greeks associated the ass with sexual licence and fertility and it was customarily sacrificed it to their god, Priapus, who was the son of Dionysus and Venus, the Goddess of Love.

Hindus believe the donkey is associated with the goddess of smallpox, perhaps as they see it as diseased and uncared for, and the Talmud contains the quote, 'If one man says to thee, 'Thou art a donkey,' pay no heed. If two speak thus, purchase a saddle'.

The Devilish Donkey

Early associations between the wild ass and the devil were contained in the *Physiologus* which is thought to have been written sometime between the 2nd and 5th centuries AD and seemed to have been based on its 'sickening cry' as Chesterton describes it. The *Physiologus* contains the passage: *Now the Devil is symbolised by this animal, for he brays about the place night and day, hour by hour, seeking his prey. He does this when he knows that the number of those who walk in darkness is equal to the number of the sons of light. For the Wild Ass does not bray unless it wants its dinner. As Job says, 'Doth the Wild Ass bray when he hath grass?' Wherefore the Apostle also: 'Our adversary the Devil, as a roaring lion, walketh about, seeking whom he may devour.'* (White 1956: 82–83)

Throughout the Middle Ages many in Western Countries practised witchcraft in which the Devil was believed to appear in the guise of a goat, stag, ram or bull. On several occasions it reportedly took the form of a black horse or pony ('ane blak galoway' in more than one Scottish transcript of proceedings) but almost never a donkey. One medieval legend does, however, feature an asinine devil. It tells of a certain Italian bishop who was persuaded by a miser to buy from him what seemed to be a very fine mule, at a quite exorbitant price. But the mule was in fact the Devil in disguise and when the Bishop rode through the city to show off his purchase it bolted into a river nearly drowning its rider. The

Bishop was only saved by the intervention of some fishermen and the story shows how Satan may buy a soul by undertaking to make him very rich in this world.

Another association between donkey and devil is found on Tarot cards, one of which depicts a devilish figure with ass ears. Although some Tarot cards are medieval in origin, however, others are more recent and it is possible that the devil-donkey design only dates from the early 20th century.

Donkey as both Christ and Devil
'The Donkey' by G K Chesterton

When fishes flew and forests walked
And figs grew upon thorn,
Some moment when the moon was blood
Then surely I was born.

With monstrous head and sickening cry
And ears like errant wings,
The devil's walking parody
On all four-footed things.

The tattered outlaw of the earth,
Of ancient crooked will;
Starve, scourge, deride me: I am dumb,
I keep my secret still.

Fools! For I also had my hour;
One far fierce hour and sweet:
There was a shout about my ears,
And palms before my feet.

A Stupid Ass
'My Donkey' by Ted Hughes

His face is what I like.
And his head, much too big for his body – a toy head,
A great, rabbit-eared pantomime head,
And his friendly rabbit face,
His big, friendly, humorous eyes – which can turn wicked,
Long and devilish, when he lays his ears back.

But mostly he's comical – and that's what I like.
I like the joke he seems
Always just about to tell me. And the laugh,
The rusty, pump-house engine that cranks up laughter
From some long-ago, far-off, laughter-less desert –

The dry, hideous guffaw
That makes his great teeth nearly fall out

Although it may seem unfair, donkeys are often shown in a silly light, or as though they're somehow ridiculous. The *Husbandman's Instructor* said of the ass that, 'the simplicity of this creature is said in history, to make Heraclitus (who always, except this time, wept for the Pride, Covetousness, and Luxury of Mankind) to laugh; for passing along very solitary, having a little before seen Luxurious Tables spread with all manner of Dainties Sea and Land could afford, he spied a poor ass contenting himself with thistles, mumbling them with as much pleasure as if he had the best provinder imaginable;

(Speed 1697:112–117) In 1845 in an equally learned prose, Low declared 'his figure, his voice, his very patience and submission, have been the subject of ridicule in every age. He has been regarded as the very emblem of stupidity, perverseness, and obstinacy, "tardus, piger, stupidus, stolidus".' (Low 1845: 437–444)

In literature the donkey has long been used to symbolise ignorance and the proverbial saying, 'the law is an ass' became popular from Dicken's Oliver Twist (1838) in which the words are spoken by Mr Bumble. In Shakespeare's 'A Midsummer Night's Dream' (c.1594) a clownish yokel, Bottom, is ridiculed by being given an ass's head and, through no fault of his own, proceeds to have an affair with Titania, queen of the fairies. In real life, Bottom was a common man with a pushy and garrulous nature but was nevertheless endearingly funny and during his romance with Titania 'the ass' comes across as ridiculous yet warm and generous-spirited, a friend to fairy and peasant alike. When the fairy queen recovers her senses she wonders at her late dotage and declares that she loathes the sight of the strange monster but Bottom's companions are genuinely sorry to see him transformed back to a human.

One Greek tale in which ass-ears are used as an insult relates that Apollo and Pan had a contest and chose Midas to decide which was the better musician. Midas favoured Pan, and Apollo, in disgust, changed his ears into those of an ass declaring, 'avarice is as deaf to the voice of virtue, as the ass to the voice of Apollo' (Lucivico Arisoto 1532 Orlando Furioso)

A number of Aesop's fables, thought to stem from the early 6th century BC, also portray the donkey as an ignorant and misguided beast. The following are examples:

Too Clever By Half

An ass crossing a river with a load of salt lost his footing and slipped into the water, so that the salt was dissolved. He was mightily pleased at finding himself relieved of his burden when he got upon his legs again. So the next time he came to a river with a load on his back, thinking that the same thing would happen if he got into the water, he let himself go under on purpose.

But this time he was loaded with sponges, which absorbed so much water that he could not keep his head up and was drowned.

There are men like the ass in this fable. They are taken by surprise when their own scheming lands them in disaster.

An Ass in a Lion's Skin (1)

An ass put on a lion's skin and went about terrifying all the brute beasts. Encountering a fox, he tried to frighten it like the rest. But the fox happened to have heard him giving tongue. 'I declare,' he said, 'I should have been scared of you myself, if I had not heard you bray.'

Uneducated men, who by putting on airs manage to pass for somebodies, often give themselves away because they cannot refrain from chattering.

An Ass in a Lion's Skin (2)

An ass put on a lion's skin, and both men and animals took him for a lion and fled from him. But when a puff of wind stripped off the skin and left him bare, everyone ran up and began to beat him with sticks and cudgels.

A poor commoner should not try to ape the style of the rich. By doing so he exposes himself to ridicule and danger; for no man can make his own what does not belong to him.

The use of lions and donkeys to symbolise wisdom and strength versus ignorance and weakness is further exemplified in the anonymus saying, 'lions led by donkeys' which was used in the First World War to describe British foot soldiers under the command of their Generals. In the same vein, a German proverb claims 'a donkey can wear a lion suit but its ear will still stick out and give it away'. An Indian tale has an ass dressed in a panther skin giving itself away by braying.

Both the French and the English call on a donkey to insult someone, 'you stupid ass' and 'comme un ane', and both nations have exported such associations to countries that they colonised. The French have an expression, 'faire le panier a deux anses' (to make a basket with two handles) which gave rise to the phrase, 'an ass with two panniers' referring to a man found walking with a lady on each arm. 'Asses as well as pitchers have ears' is an English adage meaning that children and even the stupidest of minds hear and understand many a word that the speaker assumed would pass unheeded.

The Americans, too, see the donkey as a comical soul as is inferred by the following song, the Donkey Serenade, from 1920s America: *There's a song in the air but the fair senorita doesn't seem to care for the song in the air. So I'll sing to the music if you're sure she won't think that I am just a fool serenading a mule. But try as she may in her voice there's a flaw and all that the lady can say is Hee Haw.* (Wright & Forrest 1927)

Entertainment these days is often high tech and the animated children's film, Shrek, that was released in 2001 features a humourous digital donkey. In this Hollywood invention, the ogre, Shrek, has an annoying, talking donkey who appears as a wisecracking, loudmouth sidekick of the main character and assists him in a daring quest to rescue a feisty Princess. (Dreamworks Pictures 2001) Shrek has certainly appealed to the Jaguar Formula One Grand Prix team who, during a downturn in their fortunes, raised their morale by taking a blow-up rubber donkey to all their races and photographing it trying out Formula One life. The resulting pictures can be viewed on-line on a blog at www.donkeydoesf1.co.uk. Another digital donkey appears in an early computer game, Donkey Kong, in which a princess must be saved from the clutches of a gorilla.

A Smart Ass

Although often portrayed as foolish, those that know it well argue that stubbornness in a donkey is not due to stupidity but to a highly-developed sense of self preservation. Many know from experience that it is difficult to force or frighten a donkey into doing something it sees as contrary to its own best interest. 'You must negotiate with a donkey' is a saying which seems to accord with a popular rhyme from the 19th century: 'If I had a donkey wot wouldn't go, D'ye think I'd wallop him? No no no. I'd put him in a stable and give him some hay, and the poor little donkey would go another day'.

In old English, German, Dutch or Scandinavian folk-tales each animal has its characteristic traits: the wolf personifies greed and the fox cunning. The donkey is relatively rare in these stories and many of them may derive from a time before it had been introduced to the region. Where it does occur it is probably a comparatively late substitute for some other beast and is usually shown as having great endurance and being impervious to insult and indignity because it knows that sooner or later its turn will come.

The following of Aesop's fables, the morals of which are recognised as being so true to life, also recognises a donkey's 'stupidity' as being all a facade:

One Master as Good as Another

A timid old man was grazing his donkey in a meadow when all of a sudden he was alarmed by the shouting of some enemy soldiers. 'Run for it,' he cried, 'so that they can't catch us.' But the donkey was in no hurry. 'Tell me,' said he: 'if I fall into the conqueror's hands, do you think he will make me carry a double load?' 'I shouldn't think so,' was the old man's answer. – 'Then what matter to me what master I serve as long as I only have to bear my ordinary burden?'

Moral: Poor men generally find that a change of government simply means exchanging one master for another.

George Orwell in his world-famous classic story, *Animal Farm* written in 1943 again recognises foresight and understanding in a donkey. In his book the animals on a farm rise up against their master, drive him out and attempt to run the farm themselves. All goes tragically wrong when the pigs start to assume the role and even the habits of the humans they had been so active in deposing. The novel, published just after the 2nd World War, is considered a great satire of the darker face of modern history, being a savage attack on Stalin.

Orwell includes a donkey, Benjamin, in his story to be a source of wisdom who can predict problems and remember and learn from past events. The donkey's archetypal demeanour is captured at the outset when Benjamin is described as, 'the oldest animal on the farm, and the worst tempered. He seldom talked, and when he did it was usually to make some cynical remark – for instance he would say that God had given him a tail to keep the flies off, but that he would sooner have had no tail and no flies. Alone among the animals on the farm he never laughed. If asked why, he would say that he saw nothing to laugh at. Nevertheless, without openly admitting it, he was devoted to Boxer [a cart horse]; the two of them usually spent their Sundays together in the small paddock beyond the orchard, grazing side by side and never speaking.' (Orwell 1945)

The story goes that once the animals are in charge, after the initial Rebellion, old Benjamin seemed quite unchanged: 'he did his work in the same slow obstinate way as he had done it in Jones's [the farmer's] time, never shirking and never volunteering for extra work either'. He remains calm and cynical during subsequent events and when he oversees some humans preparing to blow up a windmill that the animals have built to cut down their workload, he 'slowly, and with an air almost of amusement' nods his long muzzle. Things then go from bad to worse and result in Boxer, Benjamin's close friend, falling ill. When a van comes to take Boxer away, 'the animals were all at work weeding turnips under the supervision of a pig, when they were astonished to see Benjamin come galloping from the direction of the farm buildings, braying at the top of his voice. It was the first time that they had ever seen Benjamin excited – indeed, it was the first time that anyone had ever seen him gallop.' When the animals gather round to say goodbye to Boxer, Benjamin, being the only one able to read properly, informs them that the van is to take him to the knacker's. Years later only Benjamin, Clover, the other cart horse, Moses, the raven, and a few of the pigs can remember the Rebellion and of these only 'old Benjamin was much the same as ever, except for being a little greyer about the muzzle, and, since Boxer's death, more morose and taciturn than ever.' (Orwell 1945)

The Donkey as a Political Animal

In politics the donkey has often been invoked to ridicule a party member. Probably the best known example is its use as the American Democratic

Party symbol. This was first introduced by Thomas Nast in a cartoon in *Harper's Weekly* in 1874. The American presidential election of 2004 spawned many Democratic donkey cartoons one of which, published in *The Economist* magazine in December 2003 depicts a donkey, the Democrat Dick Gephardt, operating an amusement arcade machine to pick up and dump his rival, Howard Dean. Another, entitled 'Race to the White House', showed a donkey ridden by the Democratic candidate, Wilson, and an elephant, the symbol of the Republicans, being bitten by the mount of Ted Roosevelt.

Indeed, it is not only American politicians that receive such treatment in the Press and Dave Brown, cartoonist for *The Independent* newspaper, illustrated the pre-Christmas 2004 stalling of the Middle East Peace Process by depicting Tony Blair as a stubborn ass lead by George Bush, as Joseph, being ridden by Ariel Sharon, as a heavily pregnant Mary. A speech bubble from Bush says, 'OK … you ain't gonna give birth to no twin states … but don't let the donkey know it's just so much wind!!!'

In the Second World War William Churchill evoked a donkey in his statement, 'thus, by every device from the stick to the carrot, the emaciated Austrian donkey is made to pull the Nazi barrow up an ever-steepening hill' (Parker 2007); conversely, the German officer, Ludendorff, famously commented, 'The English soldiers fight like lions' – to which his colleague, Hoffman, replied, 'True. But don't we know that they are lions led by donkeys.' In the 21st Century, the Iraqis also signified disdain for their enemy with a donkey: their adage, 'same donkey, different saddle', has been applied both to their country's sovereign interim government set up during the recent Iraq War and to the 'Arab government with British advisers' established by British occupiers in the 1920s. Despite the recent change of 'saddle', their poor country appears no better off than before.

The Legendary Donkey

One work of fiction that has made a particular donkey into somewhat of a legend is *Travels with a Donkey in the Cevennes* written by Robert Louis Stevenson in 1878. This is an adult's book based on a true story that has established the donkey as one of the great characters in travel literature. The book documents the author's trek through the Cevennes mountain range in France with his trusty mouse-coloured donkey, Modestine. At the outset of the 12-day trip the 'haggard, drenched and despondent' Modestine is viewed as 'proof of dead stupidity, redeemed indeed by patience, but aggravated by flashes of sorry and ill-judged light-heartedness'. (Stevenson 1878)

Further quotes illustrating the Stevenson's attitude towards his donkey include: 'What that pace was, there is no word mean enough to describe; it was something as much slower than a walk as a walk is slower than a run; it kept me hanging on each foot for an incredible length of time'; 'if I dropped a few yards into the rear, or went on a few yards ahead, Modestine came instantly to a halt and began to browse'; 'of all conceivable journeys, this promised to be the most tedious'; 'long, long roads, up hill and down dale, and a pair of figures ever infinitesimally moving, foot by foot, a yard to the minute, and, like things enchanted in a nightmare, approaching no nearer to the goal.' After many humorous trials and tribulations, however, Stevenson found his disdain for Modestine turned to love and he said goodbye with much regret. (Stevenson 1878)

A lesser known donkey whose true story has also been the subject of a literary work is 'Brighty' who was a feral donkey living in the Grand Canyon in America in the 1920s. His tale is related in a children's book, *Donkey Leads the Way* written by Hiawyn Oram in 1998. 'Brighty' was discovered in his mountain cave by workmen constructing the first bridge over the Colorado River. He befriended them and became essential in carrying their building materials over the rocky terrain. The story concludes with the workers honouring their trusty pack donkey by getting him to lead the way over the bridge at its opening ceremony in 1921. (Oram 1998)

Both the above legendary donkeys reveal flashes of many of the characteristics of the imaginary donkey as described earlier in this section of the book. Their human companions appear to view them first as pitiable beasts of burden but after being increasingly reliant on them, come to think of and even treat them as equals. What this growing respect means for the future of donkeys in general will be discussed in the final chapter.

CHAPTER 10

The Future for the Donkey

It seems fitting to end this all-round tale of the donkey by assessing where it may go from here. As has always been the case, the fate of the donkey, as with any animal, is largely dependant on humans – where it is in man's best interest to keep it, it will thrive; where not, it will decline.

In the Developed World, as already described, where the donkey is a popular pet, its numbers have risen in the past few decades and, for as long as people have space to keep them, this trend looks set to continue. In America and Britain, the growing number of donkey shows and competitions is helping raising awareness of donkeys and the demand for appealing new breeds of donkey such as miniatures is increasing. As the number of healthy and well-cared for donkeys has risen in recent years, however, so has the number of neglected and unwanted animals and many of these end up in one of our rapidly expanding donkey sanctuaries. The Donkey Sanctuary

Donkey hoping for a
brighter future …

in Devon is the largest such organisation in Europe and, in addition to its role homing donkeys, it does much to promote their use as a therapy for the sick and disabled. For as long as it receives its current high level of charitable donations it will be able to benefit increasing numbers of donkeys and people and the future for its residents looks bright.

It seems, then, that the number of donkeys in Developed Countries will rise and conditions for them improve as concern for animal welfare continues and the pet business flourishes. The proven success of 'donkey therapy' means they could once again be seen as useful working animals and the search for alternative clean transport along with the opening up of canal towpaths may give them a renewed role as pack animals.

In the Developing World, the future of the donkey depends on its continued use as a working animal. Animal charities funded by First World

Countries can do much to better the treatment of donkeys by providing veterinary expertise and teaching local people how best to care for them. To secure a long-term future for donkeys, however, their value as efficient and sustainable working animals needs to be fully recognised as although most of the poorest families in rural Africa have a donkey, many farmers there only use them to carry goods and have never thought of using them to pull a plough. One charity, Oxfam Darfur, aims to change this and in co-operation with the organisation, Intermediate Technology Development Group (ITDG), is running a fund-raising campaign entitled 'How can a donkey become an ox?' This teaches people in the Kebkabiya region of Western Sudan to make lightweight ploughs suitable for donkeys. The Kebkabiya donkey plough, as it is known, has a frame made from steel pipes which attaches to a simple soft harness stuffed with straw and rags that fits comfortably round a donkey's neck. Since 1990 large numbers of local blacksmiths and farmers have been trained to manufacture and use it and it has led to crop yields increasing by 50–114 %, and the cultivated area by 86–200%. (Suliman 2005:246–256) Using donkeys for tilling the land has not only reduced drudgery for farmers and allowed them to start diversifying their crops but, by increasing yields and food security in the area, may well be partly responsible for the recent improvements in local children's health and education.

Somalia is another country where people are coming to realise the advantages of a donkey in terms of rural development and the charity, Concern, has sought to persuade farmers that to go forward they must, in one sense, go backwards. '

Most places in the world went hoe, animal and then tractor,' said agronomist, Abdullahi Abdi Yarrow. 'Somalia jumped from the hoe to tractor but now we are trying to persuade the farmers associations to move to oxen or donkeys for ploughing.

There are very few tractors available in Somalia, spare parts are extremely difficult to get and the cost of hiring them is high for impoverished farmers. One Somali villager, Moalin Abdullahi, who farms around three hectares of land and drove a tractor for 20 years is now convinced that for sustainability his oxen are better. 'If you hire a tractor you have it once – oxen you have all the time', he said. 'Tractors are very heavy and compact the soil, and the roots find it difficult to get in. Following oxen you have time to weed as you plough.' (*Elliott 2004*)

It can be thus concluded that we can be cautiously optimistic about the outlook for donkeys in rural areas of Developing Countries as long as they can be successfully re-launched as a successful model from the past with an impressive future as a four-leg drive agricultural power source.

EPILOGUE

What does the Donkey think of Us?

Having looked in some detail at how we care for the donkey, it seems appropriate to round off this book by speculating on what, if anything, it makes of us. Do we appear as a strange type of two-legged, thin-skinned, bald-faced, tail-less fellow animal with a ridiculously short neck, small head and tiny ears? In donkey terms, are we vulnerable stray foals, dominant members of the family group or rivals from another clan? As alien beings, are some of us far superior, hard-task masters to be feared and instantly obeyed while others are inexplicably attentive and gentle and seemingly happy to be ignored? In short, are we to be looked up to, thought of as equals or treated with disdain?

There is a theory that most people, instinctively but subconsciously, try to develop a similar relationship with a donkey as exists between a jenny and her foal. It would certainly benefit the human to have the donkey display the same submissive and juvenile traits as a young foal, but is it also to the donkey's advantage – and it knows it. Owning a donkey should certainly be seen as a partnership, with the owner being owned by the donkey as much as the donkey being owned by the owner.

Bibliography

ADAS Consulting Ltd (2002) *Equine Industry Welfare Guidelines Compendium for Horses, Ponies and Donkeys*

Ayto, J, ed., (2005) *Brewer's Dictionary of Phrase and Fable* 17th edn

Baker, D (1974) *Travels in a Donkey Trap* Coronet Books

Beja-Pereira, (xxxx) African Origins of the Domestic Donkey. *Science*, 304: 1781

Borwick, R (1981) *The Book of the Donkey* Pelham Books

Browning D C, ed., (1962) *Everyman's Dictionary of Quotations & Proverbs* J M Dent & Sons Ltd

Budiansky, S (1997) *The Nature of Horses: Their Evolution, Intelligence and Behaviour* Phoenix

Cartwright, Justin (2004) *The Promise of Happiness*

Chivers, K (1976) *The Shire Horse: A History of the Breed, the Society and the Men* J A Allen

Clark, Alan (1961) *The Donkeys* Pimlico

Clover P (2002) *Donkey in Distress* (Donkey Diaries) Oxford University Press

Clover P (2001) *Donkey Danger* (Donkey Diaries) Oxford University Press

Clutton-Brock, J (1992) *Horse Power: A history of the horse and the donkey in human societies*. Natural History Museum Publications

Clutton-Brock, J. (1999) *A Natural History of Domesticated Animals* 2nd edn Cambridge University Press

Cooper, J (1992) *Brewer's Book of Myth & Legend* Cassell Publishers Ltd

DEFRA (2003) 'Horse Passports – What does this mean for you?' DEFRA Publications

Dent A (1972) *Donkey: The Story of the Ass from East to West* George G Harrap & Co Ltd

Donkey Breed Society (2005) The Donkey Breed Society Stud Farms [online] Donkey Breed Society Available from: www.donkeybreedsociety.co.uk/Page.aspx?TagName=StudFarms [Date accessed: 6.05]

Donkey Breed Society (2007) *Naming Your Donkey* [online] Donkey Breed Society. Available from: www.donkeybreedsociety.co.uk/page.aspx?TagName=StudBookNaming [Date accessed: 2.12.07]

Donkey Breed Society (2007) *Stud Book Documents* [online] Donkey Breed Society. Available from: www.donkeybreedsociety.co.uk/Page.aspx?TagName=BreedingDocs [Date accessed: 2.12.07]

Donkey Breed Society (2007) *Stud Book Documents* [online] Donkey Breed Society. Available from: www.donkeybreedsociety.co.uk/page.aspx?TagName=Showing

Donkey Breed Society (2007) *Donkey Award Scheme* [online] Donkey Breed Society. Available from: www.donkeybreedsociety.co.uk/Page.aspx?TagName=ActiveDonkeys [Date accessed: 2.12.07]

Donkey Breed Society (2007) *Events Calender* [online] Donkey Breed Society. Available from: www.donkeybreedsociety.co.uk/Page.aspx?TagName=EventsCalendar [Date accessed: 2.12.07]

Dreamworks Pictures (2001) *Shrek* PDI/Dreamworks production (original score H Gregson-Williams & J Powell; based upon the book by W Steig; written by T Elliott, T Rossio, J Stillman & R S H Schulman)

Duncan, P (1992) *Zebras, Asses, and Horses: An Action Plan for the Conservation of Wild Equids* IUCN

Dunn, Douglas (2000) *The Donkey's Ears: Politovsky's Letters Home* Faber & Faber

Eadie, J (ed.) (1960) *Cruden's Popular Concordance Based on the Famous Work of Alexander Cruden* Oilphants Ltd

Elliott, Chris, (2004 Dec 24) 'We want to produce something – and will' *The Guardian*

Farmer's Weekly (1937 February 17) Classified advertisments

Fielding, D & Krause, P. (1998) *Donkeys (The Tropical Agriculturalist)* Macmillan Education Ltd

Food and Agriculture Organisation (2003) *FAO Yearbook* 57 (FAO Statistics Series no 177)

Fuller T (1732) *Gnomolgia: Adages and Proverbs*

Goodall, N (1944) *Donkey's Glory* A R Mowbray & Co

Grimshaw, A (1982) *The Horse: A Bibliography of British Books 1851–1976*

Hutchins, B & P (2002) *The Definitive Donkey: A Textbook on the Modern Ass* 2nd edn (revised and edited by Leah Patton) Hee Haw Book Service

Ireland, N O (1973) *Index to Fairy Tales, 1949–1972 including Folklore, Legends & Myths in Collections* F W Faxon Co

Kennedy, EJ (trans) (1998) Apeleius, (c.160AD) *The Golden Ass or Metamorphoses* Penguin Books

Kiple, K & Conee Ornelas, K, edn. (2000) *Cambridge World History of Food* Cambridge University Press

LiveJournal(2007)*Horrorshow*[online]LiveJournal.Availablefrom: www.livejournal.com/users/horrorshow/241052.html [Date accessed: 2.12.07]

Lloyd, A (2004 Oct 07) 'Doing the donkey work as Afghans head for polls.' *The Times*

Loftus, R & Scherf, B (1993) *World Watch List For Domestic Animal Diversity* Food and Agricultural Organization of the United Nations

Low, David (1845) *Domesticated Animals of the British Islands*

Lucivico Arisoto (1532) *Orlando Furioso*

Lunday, A (2006) *Early Bronze Age mortuary complex discovered in Syria* [online] Johns Hopkins University Office of News & Information. Available from: www.eurekalert.org/pub_releases/2006-10/jhu-eba102406.php [Date accessed 1.12.07]

McFarland, D (1981) *The Oxford Companion to Animal Behaviour* Oxford University Press

McGreevy, Paul (2004) *Equine Behaviour: A guide for veterinarians & equine scientists*

MAFF (1997) *Welfare of Animals (Transport) Order* MAFF Publications

MAFF (1990) *Welfare of Horses, Ponies & Donkeys at Markets, Sales and Fairs* MAFF Publications

Manilal, V (2004) 'India the Carrot or the Stick' *Independent on Sunday*

Mason, I. L. (1996) *A World Dictionary of Livestock Breeds, Types and Varieties* 4th edn CAB International

Milne A A (1926) *Winnie The Pooh* Methuen & Co Ltd

The Oxford Dictionary of Quotations, 2nd edn, (1953) Oxford University Press

Ogunremi (1982) *Concocting the Camels: The Economics of Transportation in Pre-Industrial Nigeria* Nok Publishers International

Oram, H (1998) *Donkey Leads the Way (Animal Heroes)* Orchard Books

Orwell, G (1945) *Animal Farm* Penguin Books

Parker, P (2007) *Donkey* [online] Webster's Online Dictionary. Available from: www.websters-online-dictionary.org/definition/DONKEY [Date accessed 2.12.07]

Payne, WJA (1990) *'Introduction to animal husbandary in the tropics,* 4th edn, Longman Scientific and Technical

Royal Veterinary College (1991) Caring for Horses, Ponies and Donkeys Part 2 (Food and Feeding)

Sankar-Oyan, R (2005) *Every donkey has its day in Arima* [online]Available from: www.trinidad-tobago.net/Article.aspx?PageId=9 [Date accessed: 2.12.07]

Speed, A (1697) *The Husbandman's Instructor*

SPANA (2008) [online] SPANA: Society for the Protection of Animals Abroad. Available from: www.spana.org/about/what_we_do.php [Date accessed 23.2.08]

Stevenson R L (1878) *Travels with a Donkey in the Cevennes*

Stevenson R L (1878) *An Inland Voyage*

Storr-Best, L (trans) (1912) *Varro on Farming*

Suliman, Mohamed Siddig (2005) 'Development of the Kebkabiya donkey plough in Western Sudan' in *Participatory Livestock Research: A Guide*, ITDG Publishing

Summerhays, R S (1970) *The Donkey Owner's Guide* Thomas Nelson & Sons Ltd

Svendsen, Dr E D (1997) 'The Donkey Sanctuary and Its Sister Charities'. In, *The Professional Handbook of the Donkey* 3rd edn. Whittet Books

Svendsen, Dr E D (1990) *Travels for a Donkey* Whittet Books

Svendsen, Dr E D (1986) *Donkey's Years* Whittet Books

Tafuri, N (2002) *The Donkey's Christmas Song* Scholastic Press

Tangye, D (1967) *A Donkey in the Meadow*

Tetlow, B (1997) 'History of the Donkey Breed Society, Showing and Judging'. In *The Professional Handbook of the Donkey* 3rd ed Whittet Books:319–334

Travelspots (2005) [online] Travelspots. Available from:www.travelspots.com/trip_tips/info/santorini_info.htm [Date accessed 6.05]

Travis, L (1990) *The Mule (Allen Breed Series)* J A Allen & Co Ltd

Treverton Jones, T (2004) *Voices of Chalford, Bisley and Bussage*

Unit for Veterinary Continuing Education (1991) *Caring for Horses, Ponies and Donkeys: Part 2 Nutrition* (Food & Feeding)

War Office Veterinary Department (1933) *Animal Management* HMSO *for the War Office'*

Warder, J T (1863) *Mule Raising*

Webster's Online Dictionary – The Rosetta Edition *www.websters-online-dictionary.org*

White T H edn. (1956) *The Book of Beasts being a translation from a Latin Bestiary of the Twelfth Century* Readers Union

Williamson, H (1952) *Donkey Boy* MacDonald & Co Ltd

Wilson, R T (1978) Studies on the livestock of Southern Darfur, Sudan VI. Notes on equines. *Trop. Anim. Hlth. Prod.* 10, 183–9

Worldlink (2007) Welcome to Worldlink [online] Worldlink Available from:www.worldlink-shanghai.com [Date accessed: 2.12.07]

Wright & Forrest (1927) 'Donkey Serenade' (music R Friml/H Stolhart words added in 1927 by B Wright/C Forrest tabulated by J Ouzts)

Index